PIANO • VOCAL • GUITAR

SING-A-LONG
Best of Christmas

❄ ❄ ❄ ❄ ❄ ❄ ❄ ❄ ❄ ❄ ❄

ISBN 978-1-4803-9301-1

HAL•LEONARD®
CORPORATION
7777 W. BLUEMOUND RD. P.O. BOX 13819 MILWAUKEE, WI 53213

Visit Hal Leonard Online at
www.halleonard.com

ALL I WANT FOR CHRISTMAS IS MY TWO FRONT TEETH

Words and Music by
DON GARDNER

BLUE CHRISTMAS

Words and Music by BILLY HAYES
and JAY JOHNSON

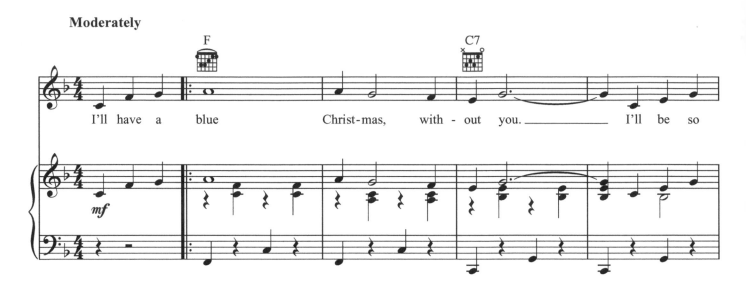

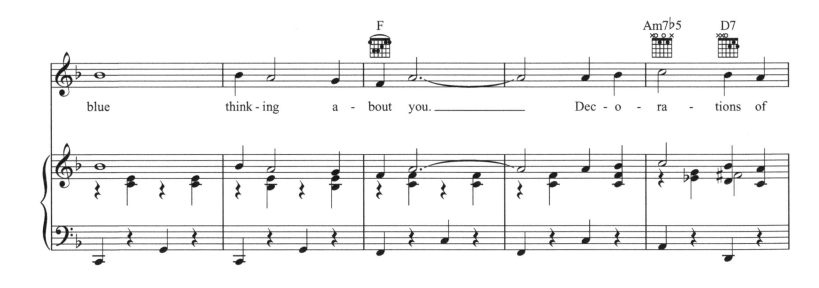

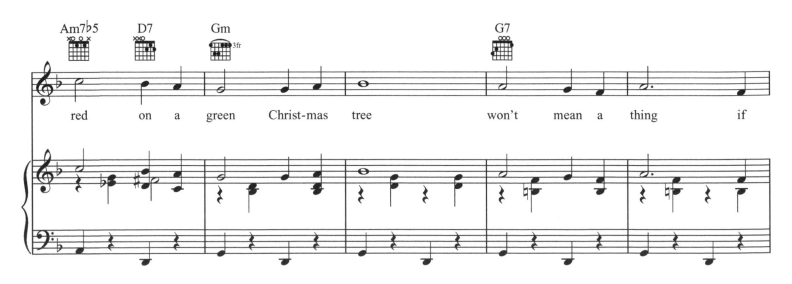

CHRISTMAS AULD LANG SYNE

Words and Music by MANN CURTIS
and FRANK MILITARY

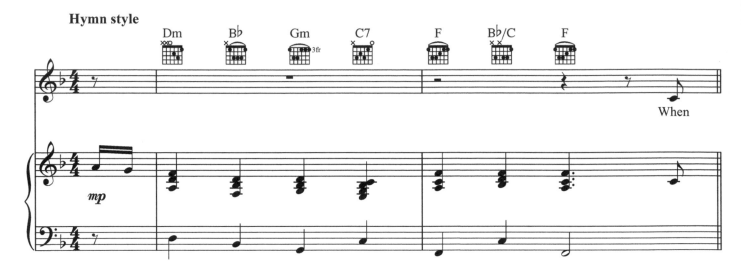

When

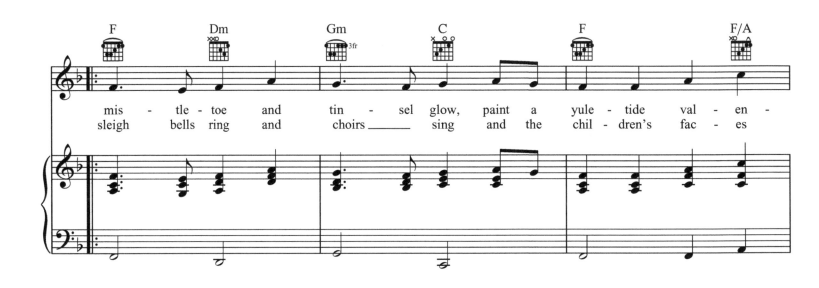

mis - tle - toe and tin - sel glow, paint a yule - tide val - en -
sleigh bells ring and choirs _____ sing and the chil - dren's fac - es

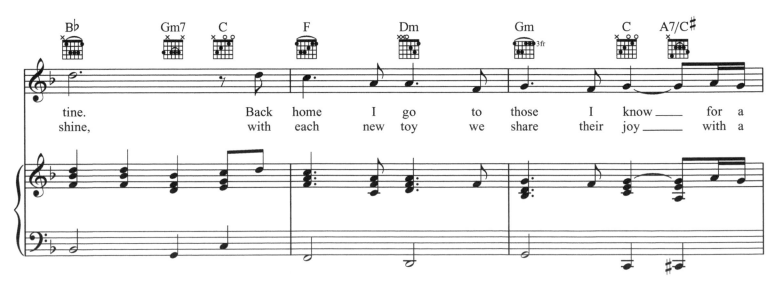

tine. Back home I go to those I know _____ for a
shine, with each new toy we share their joy _____ with a

CHRISTMAS IN KILLARNEY

Words and Music by JOHN REDMOND
and FRANK WELDON

CHRISTMAS TIME IS HERE
from A CHARLIE BROWN CHRISTMAS

Words by LEE MENDELSON
Music by VINCE GUARALDI

THE CHRISTMAS WALTZ

Words by SAMMY CAHN
Music by JULE STYNE

Frost-ed win-dow-panes, can-dles gleam-ing in-side, paint-ed can-dy canes on the tree; San-ta's on his way, he's filled his

sleigh with things, _____ things for you and for

me. It's that time of year, _____ when the world falls in

love, ev - 'ry song you hear _____ seems to say: _____

_____ "Mer - ry Christ - mas, _____ may your New Year

FELIZ NAVIDAD

Music and Lyrics by
JOSÉ FELICIANO

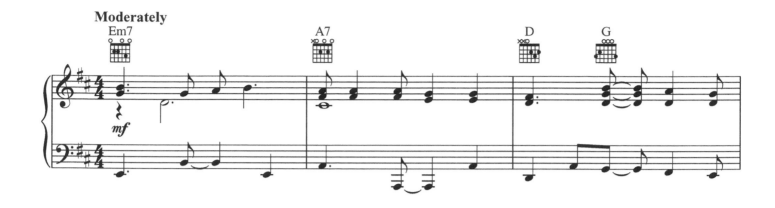

HAVE YOURSELF A MERRY LITTLE CHRISTMAS

from MEET ME IN ST. LOUIS

Words and Music by HUGH MARTIN
and RALPH BLANE

Lyrics: When the stee-ple bells sound their "A," they don't play it in tune.

IT'S BEGINNING TO LOOK LIKE CHRISTMAS

By MEREDITH WILLSON

To Coda

THE LITTLE DRUMMER BOY

Words and Music by HARRY SIMEONE,
HENRY ONORATI and KATHERINE DAVIS

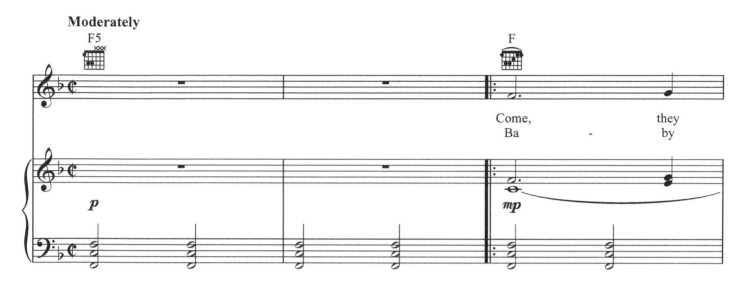

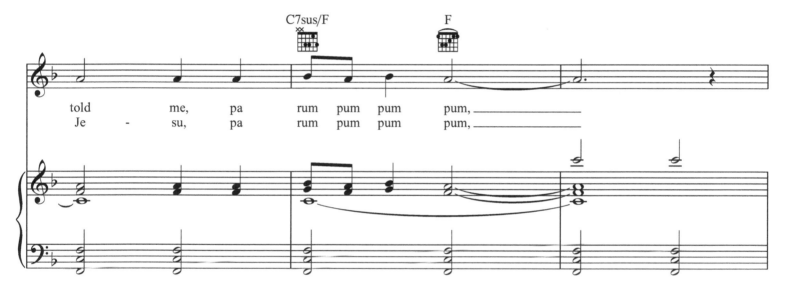

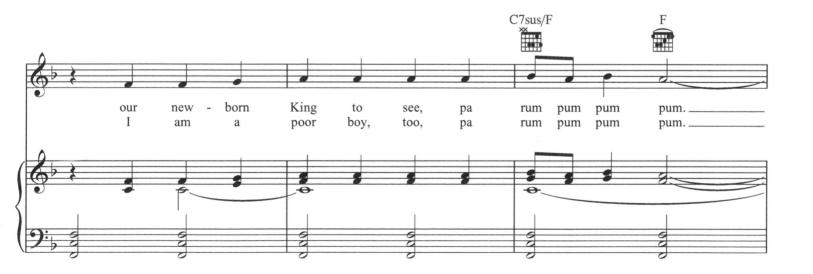

LITTLE SAINT NICK

Words and Music by BRIAN WILSON
and MIKE LOVE

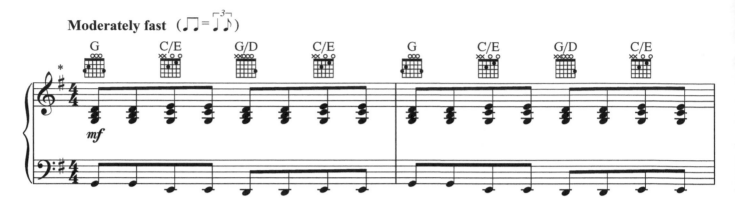

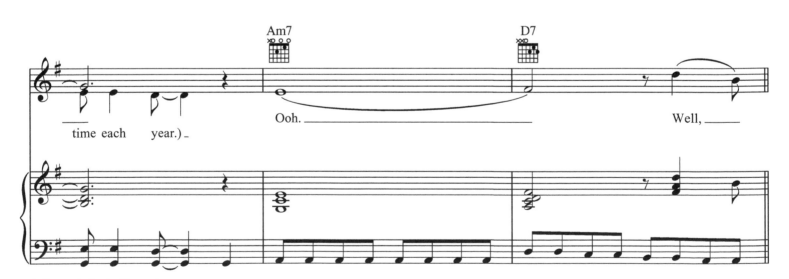

* *Recorded a half step lower.*

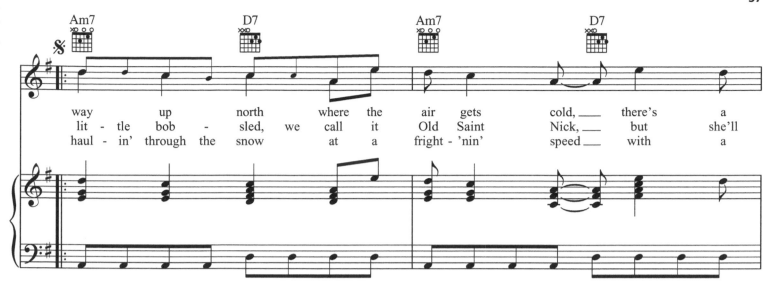

way up north where the air gets cold, ___ there's a
lit - tle bob - sled, we call it Old Saint Nick, ___ but she'll
haul - in' through the snow at a fright - 'nin' speed ___ with a

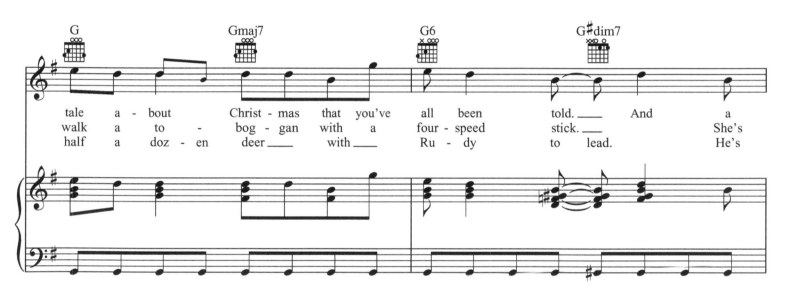

tale a - bout Christ - mas that you've all been told. ___ And a
walk a to - bog - gan with a four - speed stick. ___ She's
half a doz - en deer ___ with ___ Ru - dy to lead. He's

real fa - mous cat all dressed up in red, ___ and he
can - dy ap - ple red with a ski for a wheel, and when
got - ta wear his gog - gles 'cause the snow real - ly flies, and he's

A MARSHMALLOW WORLD

Words by CARL SIGMAN
Music by PETER DE ROSE

Lyrics for
Sing-A-Long Best of Christmas

All I Want for Christmas Is My Two Front Teeth

Everybody stops and stares at me.
These two teeth are gone, as you can see.
I don't know just who to blame for this catastrophe!
But my one wish for Christmas Eve is as plain as
    it can be!

All I want for Christmas is my two front teeth,
My two front teeth, see, my two front teeth!
Gee, if I could only have my two front teeth,
Then I could wish you, "Merry Christmas!"

It seems so long since I could say,
"Sister Susie sitting on a thistle!"
Gosh, oh gee, how happy I'd be,
If I could only whistle.

All I want for Christmas is my two front teeth,
My two front teeth, see, my two front teeth!
Gee, if I could only have my two front teeth,
Then I could wish you, "Merry Christmas!"

Blue Christmas

I'll have a blue Christmas, without you.
I'll be so blue thinking about you.
Decorations of red on a green Christmas tree
Won't mean a thing if you're not here with me.
I'll have a blue Christmas, that's certain.
And when that blue heartache starts hurtin',
You'll be doin' alright, with your Christmas of white,
But I'll have a blue, blue Christmas.

Christmas Auld Lang Syne

When mistletoe and tinsel glow,
Paint a yuletide valentine.
Back home I go to those I know
For a Christmas auld lang syne.
And as we gather 'round the tree,
Our voices all combine
In sweet accord to thank the Lord
For a Christmas auld lang syne.

When sleigh bells ring and choirs sing
And the children's faces shine,
With each new toy we share their joy
With a Christmas auld lang syne.
We sing His praise this day of days
And pray next year this time
We'll all be near to share the cheer
Of a Christmas auld lang syne.

Christmas in Killarney

Christmas in Killarney is wonderful to see.
Listen to my story and I'll take you back with me.

The holly green, the ivy green,
The prettiest picture you've ever seen
Is Christmas in Killarney
With all of the folks at home.

It's nice to know, to kiss your beau
While cuddling under the mistletoe,
And Santa Claus, you know of course,
Is one of the boys from home.

The door is always open,
The neighbors pay a call,
And Father John, before he's gone,
Will bless the house and all.

How grand it feels to click your heels
And join in the fun of the jigs and reels.
I'm handing you no blarney,
The likes you've never known
Is Christmas in Killarney,
With all of the folks at home.

Christmas Time Is Here

Christmas time is here,
Happiness and cheer.
Fun for all that children call
Their favorite time of year.

Snowflakes in the air,
Carols everywhere.
Olden times and ancient rhymes
Of love and dreams to share.

Sleighbells in the air,
Beauty everywhere.
Yuletide by the fireside
And joyful memories there.
Christmas time is here,
We'll be drawing near.
Oh, that we could always see
Such spirit through the year.

The Christmas Waltz

Frosted window panes,
Candles gleaming inside,
Painted candy canes on the tree;
Santa's on his way,
He's filled his sleigh with things,
Things for you and for me.

It's that time of year,
When the world falls in love,
Every song you hear seems to say:
"Merry Christmas,
May your New Year dreams come true."
And this song of mine,
In three-quarter time,
Wishes you and yours
The same thing too.

Feliz Navidad

Feliz Navidad.
Feliz Navidad.
Feliz Navidad.
Próspero año y felicidad.

Feliz Navidad.
Feliz Navidad.
Feliz Navidad.
Próspero año y felicidad.

I want to wish you a Merry Christmas,
With lots of presents to make you happy.
I want to wish you a Merry Christmas
From the bottom of my heart.

I want to wish you a Merry Christmas,
With mistletoe and lots of cheer,
With lots of laughter throughout the years,
From the bottom of my heart.

Feliz Navidad.
Feliz Navidad.
Feliz Navidad.
Próspero año y felicidad.

Have Yourself a Merry Little Christmas

When the steeple bells sound their "A,"
They don't play it in tune.
But the welkin will ring one day,
And that day will be soon.

Have yourself a merry little Christmas,
Let your heart be light.
From now on our troubles will be out of sight.
Have yourself a merry little Christmas,
Make the Yuletide gay.
From now on our troubles will be miles away.
Here we are as in olden days,
Happy golden days of yore.
Faithful friends who are dear to us
Gather near to us once more.
Through the years we all will be together
If the fates allow.
Hang a shining star upon the highest bough,
And have yourself a merry little Christmas now.

Here we are as in olden days,
Happy golden days of yore.
Faithful friends who are dear to us
Gather near to us once more.
Through the years we all will be together
If the fates allow.
Hang a shining star upon the highest bough,
And have yourself a merry little Christmas now.

It's Beginning to Look Like Christmas

It's beginning to look a lot like Christmas,
Everywhere you go.
Take a look in the five and ten,
Glistening once again,
With candy canes and silver lanes aglow.

It's beginning to look a lot like Christmas,
Toys in every store.
But the prettiest sight to see
Is the holly that will be
On your own front door.

A pair of hopalong boots
And a pistol that shoots
Is the wish of Barney and Ben.
Dolls that will talk
And will go for a walk
Is the hope of Janice and Jen;
And Mom and Dad can hardly wait
For school to start again.

It's beginning to look a lot like Christmas,
Everywhere you go.
There's a tree in the grand hotel,
One in the park as well,
The sturdy kind that doesn't mind a snow.

It's beginning to look a lot like Christmas,
Soon the bells will start.
And the thing that will make them ring
Is the carol that you sing
Right within your heart.

The Little Drummer Boy

Come, they told me, pa rum pum pum pum.
Our newborn King to see, pa rum pum pum pum.
Our finest gifts we bring, pa rum pum pum pum,
To lay before the King, pa rum pum pum pum,
Rum pum pum pum, rum pum pum pum.
So to honor Him, pa rum pum pum pum,
When we come.

Baby Jesu, pa rum pum pum pum.
I am a poor boy, too, pa rum pum pum pum.
I have no gift to bring, pa rum pum pum pum,
That's fit to give our King, pa rum pum pum pum,
Rum pum pum pum, rum pum pum pum.
Shall I play for you, pa rum pum pum pum,
On my drum?

Mary nodded, pa rum pum pum pum.
The ox and lamb kept time, pa rum pum pum pum.
I played my drum for Him, pa rum pum pum pum.
I played my best for Him, pa rum pum pum pum,
Rum pum pum pum, rum pum pum pum.
Then He smiled at me, pa rum pum pum pum,
Me and my drum.

Little Saint Nick

Ooh, Merry Christmas, Saint Nick. Ooh.
(Christmas comes this time each year.)

Well, way up north where the air gets cold,
There's a tale about Christmas that you've
   all been told.
And a real famous cat all dressed up in red,
And he spends the whole year workin' out
   on his sled.

It's the Little Saint Nick. (Little Saint Nick.)
It's the Little Saint Nick. (Little Saint Nick.)

Just a little bobsled, we call it Old Saint Nick,
But she'll walk a toboggan with a four-speed stick.
She's candy-apple red with a ski for a wheel,
And when Santa hits the gas, man, just watch
   her peel.

It's the Little Saint Nick. (Little Saint Nick.)
It's the Little Saint Nick. (Little Saint Nick.)

Lyrics for
Sing-A-Long Best of Christmas

All I Want for Christmas Is My Two Front Teeth

Everybody stops and stares at me.
These two teeth are gone, as you can see.
I don't know just who to blame for this catastrophe!
But my one wish for Christmas Eve is as plain as
  it can be!

All I want for Christmas is my two front teeth,
My two front teeth, see, my two front teeth!
Gee, if I could only have my two front teeth,
Then I could wish you, "Merry Christmas!"

It seems so long since I could say,
"Sister Susie sitting on a thistle!"
Gosh, oh gee, how happy I'd be,
If I could only whistle.

All I want for Christmas is my two front teeth,
My two front teeth, see, my two front teeth!
Gee, if I could only have my two front teeth,
Then I could wish you, "Merry Christmas!"

Blue Christmas

I'll have a blue Christmas, without you.
I'll be so blue thinking about you.
Decorations of red on a green Christmas tree
Won't mean a thing if you're not here with me.
I'll have a blue Christmas, that's certain.
And when that blue heartache starts hurtin',
You'll be doin' alright, with your Christmas of white,
But I'll have a blue, blue Christmas.

Christmas Auld Lang Syne

When mistletoe and tinsel glow,
Paint a yuletide valentine.
Back home I go to those I know
For a Christmas auld lang syne.
And as we gather 'round the tree,
Our voices all combine
In sweet accord to thank the Lord
For a Christmas auld lang syne.

When sleigh bells ring and choirs sing
And the children's faces shine,
With each new toy we share their joy
With a Christmas auld lang syne.
We sing His praise this day of days
And pray next year this time
We'll all be near to share the cheer
Of a Christmas auld lang syne.

Christmas in Killarney

Christmas in Killarney is wonderful to see.
Listen to my story and I'll take you back with me.

The holly green, the ivy green,
The prettiest picture you've ever seen
Is Christmas in Killarney
With all of the folks at home.

It's nice to know, to kiss your beau
While cuddling under the mistletoe,
And Santa Claus, you know of course,
Is one of the boys from home.

The door is always open,
The neighbors pay a call,
And Father John, before he's gone,
Will bless the house and all.

How grand it feels to click your heels
And join in the fun of the jigs and reels.
I'm handing you no blarney,
The likes you've never known
Is Christmas in Killarney,
With all of the folks at home.

Christmas Time Is Here

Christmas time is here,
Happiness and cheer.
Fun for all that children call
Their favorite time of year.

Snowflakes in the air,
Carols everywhere.
Olden times and ancient rhymes
Of love and dreams to share.

Sleighbells in the air,
Beauty everywhere.
Yuletide by the fireside
And joyful memories there.
Christmas time is here,
We'll be drawing near.
Oh, that we could always see
Such spirit through the year.

The Christmas Waltz

Frosted window panes,
Candles gleaming inside,
Painted candy canes on the tree;
Santa's on his way,
He's filled his sleigh with things,
Things for you and for me.

It's that time of year,
When the world falls in love,
Every song you hear seems to say:
"Merry Christmas,
May your New Year dreams come true."
And this song of mine,
In three-quarter time,
Wishes you and yours
The same thing too.

Feliz Navidad

Feliz Navidad.
Feliz Navidad.
Feliz Navidad.
Próspero año y felicidad.

Feliz Navidad.
Feliz Navidad.
Feliz Navidad.
Próspero año y felicidad.

I want to wish you a Merry Christmas,
With lots of presents to make you happy.
I want to wish you a Merry Christmas
From the bottom of my heart.

I want to wish you a Merry Christmas,
With mistletoe and lots of cheer,
With lots of laughter throughout the years,
From the bottom of my heart.

Feliz Navidad.
Feliz Navidad.
Feliz Navidad.
Próspero año y felicidad.

Music and Lyrics by José Feliciano
Copyright © 1970 J & H Publishing Company (ASCAP)
Copyright Renewed
All Rights Administered by Law, P.A. o/b/o J & H Publishing Company

Have Yourself a Merry Little Christmas

When the steeple bells sound their "A,"
They don't play it in tune.
But the welkin will ring one day,
And that day will be soon.

Have yourself a merry little Christmas,
Let your heart be light.
From now on our troubles will be out of sight.
Have yourself a merry little Christmas,
Make the Yuletide gay.
From now on our troubles will be miles away.
Here we are as in olden days,
Happy golden days of yore.
Faithful friends who are dear to us
Gather near to us once more.
Through the years we all will be together
If the fates allow.
Hang a shining star upon the highest bough,
And have yourself a merry little Christmas now.

Here we are as in olden days,
Happy golden days of yore.
Faithful friends who are dear to us
Gather near to us once more.
Through the years we all will be together
If the fates allow.
Hang a shining star upon the highest bough,
And have yourself a merry little Christmas now.

Words and Music by Hugh Martin and Ralph Blane
© 1943 (Renewed) METRO-GOLDWYN-MAYER INC.
© 1944 (Renewed) EMI FEIST CATALOG INC.
All Rights Controlled and Administered by EMI FEIST CATALOG INC. (Publishing) and ALFRED MUSIC (Print)

It's Beginning to Look Like Christmas

It's beginning to look a lot like Christmas,
Everywhere you go.
Take a look in the five and ten,
Glistening once again,
With candy canes and silver lanes aglow.

It's beginning to look a lot like Christmas,
Toys in every store.
But the prettiest sight to see
Is the holly that will be
On your own front door.

A pair of hopalong boots
And a pistol that shoots
Is the wish of Barney and Ben.
Dolls that will talk
And will go for a walk
Is the hope of Janice and Jen;
And Mom and Dad can hardly wait
For school to start again.

It's beginning to look a lot like Christmas,
Everywhere you go.
There's a tree in the grand hotel,
One in the park as well,
The sturdy kind that doesn't mind a snow.

It's beginning to look a lot like Christmas,
Soon the bells will start.
And the thing that will make them ring
Is the carol that you sing
Right within your heart.

By Meredith Willson
© 1951 PLYMOUTH MUSIC CO., INC.
© Renewed 1979 FRANK MUSIC CORP. and MEREDITH WILLSON MUSIC

The Little Drummer Boy

Come, they told me, pa rum pum pum pum.
Our newborn King to see, pa rum pum pum pum.
Our finest gifts we bring, pa rum pum pum pum,
To lay before the King, pa rum pum pum pum,
Rum pum pum pum, rum pum pum pum.
So to honor Him, pa rum pum pum pum,
When we come.

Baby Jesu, pa rum pum pum pum.
I am a poor boy, too, pa rum pum pum pum.
I have no gift to bring, pa rum pum pum pum,
That's fit to give our King, pa rum pum pum pum,
Rum pum pum pum, rum pum pum pum.
Shall I play for you, pa rum pum pum pum,
On my drum?

Mary nodded, pa rum pum pum pum.
The ox and lamb kept time, pa rum pum pum pum.
I played my drum for Him, pa rum pum pum pum.
I played my best for Him, pa rum pum pum pum,
Rum pum pum pum, rum pum pum pum.
Then He smiled at me, pa rum pum pum pum,
Me and my drum.

Words and Music by Harry Simeone, Henry Onorati and Katherine Davis
© 1958 (Renewed) EMI MILLS MUSIC, INC. and INTERNATIONAL KORWIN CORP.
Worldwide Print Rights Administered by ALFRED MUSIC

Little Saint Nick

Ooh, Merry Christmas, Saint Nick. Ooh.
(Christmas comes this time each year.)

Well, way up north where the air gets cold,
There's a tale about Christmas that you've
    all been told.
And a real famous cat all dressed up in red,
And he spends the whole year workin' out
    on his sled.

It's the Little Saint Nick. (Little Saint Nick.)
It's the Little Saint Nick. (Little Saint Nick.)

Just a little bobsled, we call it Old Saint Nick,
But she'll walk a toboggan with a four-speed stick.
She's candy-apple red with a ski for a wheel,
And when Santa hits the gas, man, just watch
    her peel.

It's the Little Saint Nick. (Little Saint Nick.)
It's the Little Saint Nick. (Little Saint Nick.)

❄ ❄ ❄ ❄ ❄ ❄ ❄ ❄ ❄ ❄ ❄ ❄

Lyrics for
Sing-A-Long Best of Christmas

All I Want for Christmas Is My Two Front Teeth

Everybody stops and stares at me.
These two teeth are gone, as you can see.
I don't know just who to blame for this catastrophe!
But my one wish for Christmas Eve is as plain as
it can be!

All I want for Christmas is my two front teeth,
My two front teeth, see, my two front teeth!
Gee, if I could only have my two front teeth,
Then I could wish you, "Merry Christmas!"

It seems so long since I could say,
"Sister Susie sitting on a thistle!"
Gosh, oh gee, how happy I'd be,
If I could only whistle.

All I want for Christmas is my two front teeth,
My two front teeth, see, my two front teeth!
Gee, if I could only have my two front teeth,
Then I could wish you, "Merry Christmas!"

Blue Christmas

I'll have a blue Christmas, without you.
I'll be so blue thinking about you.
Decorations of red on a green Christmas tree
Won't mean a thing if you're not here with me.
I'll have a blue Christmas, that's certain.
And when that blue heartache starts hurtin',
You'll be doin' alright, with your Christmas of white,
But I'll have a blue, blue Christmas.

Christmas Auld Lang Syne

When mistletoe and tinsel glow,
Paint a yuletide valentine.
Back home I go to those I know
For a Christmas auld lang syne.
And as we gather 'round the tree,
Our voices all combine
In sweet accord to thank the Lord
For a Christmas auld lang syne.

When sleigh bells ring and choirs sing
And the children's faces shine,
With each new toy we share their joy
With a Christmas auld lang syne.
We sing His praise this day of days
And pray next year this time
We'll all be near to share the cheer
Of a Christmas auld lang syne.

Christmas in Killarney

Christmas in Killarney is wonderful to see.
Listen to my story and I'll take you back with me.

The holly green, the ivy green,
The prettiest picture you've ever seen
Is Christmas in Killarney
With all of the folks at home.

It's nice to know, to kiss your beau
While cuddling under the mistletoe,
And Santa Claus, you know of course,
Is one of the boys from home.

The door is always open,
The neighbors pay a call,
And Father John, before he's gone,
Will bless the house and all.

How grand it feels to click your heels
And join in the fun of the jigs and reels.
I'm handing you no blarney,
The likes you've never known
Is Christmas in Killarney,
With all of the folks at home.

Christmas Time Is Here

Christmas time is here,
Happiness and cheer.
Fun for all that children call
Their favorite time of year.

Snowflakes in the air,
Carols everywhere.
Olden times and ancient rhymes
Of love and dreams to share.

Sleighbells in the air,
Beauty everywhere.
Yuletide by the fireside
And joyful memories there.
Christmas time is here,
We'll be drawing near.
Oh, that we could always see
Such spirit through the year.

The Christmas Waltz

Frosted window panes,
Candles gleaming inside,
Painted candy canes on the tree;
Santa's on his way,
He's filled his sleigh with things,
Things for you and for me.

It's that time of year,
When the world falls in love,
Every song you hear seems to say:
"Merry Christmas,
May your New Year dreams come true."
And this song of mine,
In three-quarter time,
Wishes you and yours
The same thing too.

Feliz Navidad

Feliz Navidad.
Feliz Navidad.
Feliz Navidad.
Próspero año y felicidad.

Feliz Navidad.
Feliz Navidad.
Feliz Navidad.
Próspero año y felicidad.

I want to wish you a Merry Christmas,
With lots of presents to make you happy.
I want to wish you a Merry Christmas
From the bottom of my heart.

I want to wish you a Merry Christmas,
With mistletoe and lots of cheer,
With lots of laughter throughout the years,
From the bottom of my heart.

Feliz Navidad.
Feliz Navidad.
Feliz Navidad.
Próspero año y felicidad.

Have Yourself a Merry Little Christmas

When the steeple bells sound their "A,"
They don't play it in tune.
But the welkin will ring one day,
And that day will be soon.

Have yourself a merry little Christmas,
Let your heart be light.
From now on our troubles will be out of sight.
Have yourself a merry little Christmas,
Make the Yuletide gay.
From now on our troubles will be miles away.
Here we are as in olden days,
Happy golden days of yore.
Faithful friends who are dear to us
Gather near to us once more.
Through the years we all will be together
If the fates allow.
Hang a shining star upon the highest bough,
And have yourself a merry little Christmas now.

Here we are as in olden days,
Happy golden days of yore.
Faithful friends who are dear to us
Gather near to us once more.
Through the years we all will be together
If the fates allow.
Hang a shining star upon the highest bough,
And have yourself a merry little Christmas now.

It's Beginning to Look Like Christmas

It's beginning to look a lot like Christmas,
Everywhere you go.
Take a look in the five and ten,
Glistening once again,
With candy canes and silver lanes aglow.

It's beginning to look a lot like Christmas,
Toys in every store.
But the prettiest sight to see
Is the holly that will be
On your own front door.

A pair of hopalong boots
And a pistol that shoots
Is the wish of Barney and Ben.
Dolls that will talk
And will go for a walk
Is the hope of Janice and Jen;
And Mom and Dad can hardly wait
For school to start again.

It's beginning to look a lot like Christmas,
Everywhere you go.
There's a tree in the grand hotel,
One in the park as well,
The sturdy kind that doesn't mind a snow.

It's beginning to look a lot like Christmas,
Soon the bells will start.
And the thing that will make them ring
Is the carol that you sing
Right within your heart.

The Little Drummer Boy

Come, they told me, pa rum pum pum pum.
Our newborn King to see, pa rum pum pum pum.
Our finest gifts we bring, pa rum pum pum pum,
To lay before the King, pa rum pum pum pum,
Rum pum pum pum, rum pum pum pum.
So to honor Him, pa rum pum pum pum,
When we come.

Baby Jesu, pa rum pum pum pum.
I am a poor boy, too, pa rum pum pum pum.
I have no gift to bring, pa rum pum pum pum,
That's fit to give our King, pa rum pum pum pum,
Rum pum pum pum, rum pum pum pum.
Shall I play for you, pa rum pum pum pum,
On my drum?

Mary nodded, pa rum pum pum pum.
The ox and lamb kept time, pa rum pum pum pum.
I played my drum for Him, pa rum pum pum pum.
I played my best for Him, pa rum pum pum pum,
Rum pum pum pum, rum pum pum pum.
Then He smiled at me, pa rum pum pum pum,
Me and my drum.

Little Saint Nick

Ooh, Merry Christmas, Saint Nick. Ooh.
(Christmas comes this time each year.)

Well, way up north where the air gets cold,
There's a tale about Christmas that you've
   all been told.
And a real famous cat all dressed up in red,
And he spends the whole year workin' out
   on his sled.

It's the Little Saint Nick. (Little Saint Nick.)
It's the Little Saint Nick. (Little Saint Nick.)

Just a little bobsled, we call it Old Saint Nick,
But she'll walk a toboggan with a four-speed stick.
She's candy-apple red with a ski for a wheel,
And when Santa hits the gas, man, just watch
   her peel.

It's the Little Saint Nick. (Little Saint Nick.)
It's the Little Saint Nick. (Little Saint Nick.)

❄ ❄ ❄ ❄ ❄ ❄ ❄ ❄ ❄ ❄ ❄

Lyrics for
Sing-A-Long Best of Christmas

All I Want for Christmas Is My Two Front Teeth

Everybody stops and stares at me.
These two teeth are gone, as you can see.
I don't know just who to blame for this catastrophe!
But my one wish for Christmas Eve is as plain as
  it can be!

All I want for Christmas is my two front teeth,
My two front teeth, see, my two front teeth!
Gee, if I could only have my two front teeth,
Then I could wish you, "Merry Christmas!"

It seems so long since I could say,
"Sister Susie sitting on a thistle!"
Gosh, oh gee, how happy I'd be,
If I could only whistle.

All I want for Christmas is my two front teeth,
My two front teeth, see, my two front teeth!
Gee, if I could only have my two front teeth,
Then I could wish you, "Merry Christmas!"

Blue Christmas

I'll have a blue Christmas, without you.
I'll be so blue thinking about you.
Decorations of red on a green Christmas tree
Won't mean a thing if you're not here with me.
I'll have a blue Christmas, that's certain.
And when that blue heartache starts hurtin',
You'll be doin' alright, with your Christmas of white,
But I'll have a blue, blue Christmas.

Christmas Auld Lang Syne

When mistletoe and tinsel glow,
Paint a yuletide valentine.
Back home I go to those I know
For a Christmas auld lang syne.
And as we gather 'round the tree,
Our voices all combine
In sweet accord to thank the Lord
For a Christmas auld lang syne.

When sleigh bells ring and choirs sing
And the children's faces shine,
With each new toy we share their joy
With a Christmas auld lang syne.
We sing His praise this day of days
And pray next year this time
We'll all be near to share the cheer
Of a Christmas auld lang syne.

Christmas in Killarney

Christmas in Killarney is wonderful to see.
Listen to my story and I'll take you back with me.

The holly green, the ivy green,
The prettiest picture you've ever seen
Is Christmas in Killarney
With all of the folks at home.

It's nice to know, to kiss your beau
While cuddling under the mistletoe,
And Santa Claus, you know of course,
Is one of the boys from home.

The door is always open,
The neighbors pay a call,
And Father John, before he's gone,
Will bless the house and all.

How grand it feels to click your heels
And join in the fun of the jigs and reels.
I'm handing you no blarney,
The likes you've never known
Is Christmas in Killarney,
With all of the folks at home.

Christmas Time Is Here

Christmas time is here,
Happiness and cheer.
Fun for all that children call
Their favorite time of year.

Snowflakes in the air,
Carols everywhere.
Olden times and ancient rhymes
Of love and dreams to share.

Sleighbells in the air,
Beauty everywhere.
Yuletide by the fireside
And joyful memories there.
Christmas time is here,
We'll be drawing near.
Oh, that we could always see
Such spirit through the year.

The Christmas Waltz

Frosted window panes,
Candles gleaming inside,
Painted candy canes on the tree;
Santa's on his way,
He's filled his sleigh with things,
Things for you and for me.

It's that time of year,
When the world falls in love,
Every song you hear seems to say:
"Merry Christmas,
May your New Year dreams come true."
And this song of mine,
In three-quarter time,
Wishes you and yours
The same thing too.

Feliz Navidad

Feliz Navidad.
Feliz Navidad.
Feliz Navidad.
Próspero año y felicidad.

Feliz Navidad.
Feliz Navidad.
Feliz Navidad.
Próspero año y felicidad.

I want to wish you a Merry Christmas,
With lots of presents to make you happy.
I want to wish you a Merry Christmas
From the bottom of my heart.

I want to wish you a Merry Christmas,
With mistletoe and lots of cheer,
With lots of laughter throughout the years,
From the bottom of my heart.

Feliz Navidad.
Feliz Navidad.
Feliz Navidad.
Próspero año y felicidad.

Have Yourself a Merry Little Christmas

When the steeple bells sound their "A,"
They don't play it in tune.
But the welkin will ring one day,
And that day will be soon.

Have yourself a merry little Christmas,
Let your heart be light.
From now on our troubles will be out of sight.
Have yourself a merry little Christmas,
Make the Yuletide gay.
From now on our troubles will be miles away.
Here we are as in olden days,
Happy golden days of yore.
Faithful friends who are dear to us
Gather near to us once more.
Through the years we all will be together
If the fates allow.
Hang a shining star upon the highest bough,
And have yourself a merry little Christmas now.

Here we are as in olden days,
Happy golden days of yore.
Faithful friends who are dear to us
Gather near to us once more.
Through the years we all will be together
If the fates allow.
Hang a shining star upon the highest bough,
And have yourself a merry little Christmas now.

It's Beginning to Look Like Christmas

It's beginning to look a lot like Christmas,
Everywhere you go.
Take a look in the five and ten,
Glistening once again,
With candy canes and silver lanes aglow.

It's beginning to look a lot like Christmas,
Toys in every store.
But the prettiest sight to see
Is the holly that will be
On your own front door.

A pair of hopalong boots
And a pistol that shoots
Is the wish of Barney and Ben.
Dolls that will talk
And will go for a walk
Is the hope of Janice and Jen;
And Mom and Dad can hardly wait
For school to start again.

It's beginning to look a lot like Christmas,
Everywhere you go.
There's a tree in the grand hotel,
One in the park as well,
The sturdy kind that doesn't mind a snow.

It's beginning to look a lot like Christmas,
Soon the bells will start.
And the thing that will make them ring
Is the carol that you sing
Right within your heart.

The Little Drummer Boy

Come, they told me, pa rum pum pum pum.
Our newborn King to see, pa rum pum pum pum.
Our finest gifts we bring, pa rum pum pum pum,
To lay before the King, pa rum pum pum pum,
Rum pum pum pum, rum pum pum pum.
So to honor Him, pa rum pum pum pum,
When we come.

Baby Jesu, pa rum pum pum pum.
I am a poor boy, too, pa rum pum pum pum.
I have no gift to bring, pa rum pum pum pum,
That's fit to give our King, pa rum pum pum pum,
Rum pum pum pum, rum pum pum pum.
Shall I play for you, pa rum pum pum pum,
On my drum?

Mary nodded, pa rum pum pum pum.
The ox and lamb kept time, pa rum pum pum pum.
I played my drum for Him, pa rum pum pum pum.
I played my best for Him, pa rum pum pum pum,
Rum pum pum pum, rum pum pum pum.
Then He smiled at me, pa rum pum pum pum,
Me and my drum.

Little Saint Nick

Ooh, Merry Christmas, Saint Nick. Ooh.
(Christmas comes this time each year.)

Well, way up north where the air gets cold,
There's a tale about Christmas that you've
   all been told.
And a real famous cat all dressed up in red,
And he spends the whole year workin' out
   on his sled.

It's the Little Saint Nick. (Little Saint Nick.)
It's the Little Saint Nick. (Little Saint Nick.)

Just a little bobsled, we call it Old Saint Nick,
But she'll walk a toboggan with a four-speed stick.
She's candy-apple red with a ski for a wheel,
And when Santa hits the gas, man, just watch
   her peel.

It's the Little Saint Nick. (Little Saint Nick.)
It's the Little Saint Nick. (Little Saint Nick.)

❄ ❄ ❄ ❄ ❄ ❄ ❄ ❄ ❄ ❄ ❄

Lyrics for
Sing-A-Long Best of Christmas

All I Want for Christmas Is My Two Front Teeth

Everybody stops and stares at me.
These two teeth are gone, as you can see.
I don't know just who to blame for this catastrophe!
But my one wish for Christmas Eve is as plain as
  it can be!

All I want for Christmas is my two front teeth,
My two front teeth, see, my two front teeth!
Gee, if I could only have my two front teeth,
Then I could wish you, "Merry Christmas!"

It seems so long since I could say,
"Sister Susie sitting on a thistle!"
Gosh, oh gee, how happy I'd be,
If I could only whistle.

All I want for Christmas is my two front teeth,
My two front teeth, see, my two front teeth!
Gee, if I could only have my two front teeth,
Then I could wish you, "Merry Christmas!"

Blue Christmas

I'll have a blue Christmas, without you.
I'll be so blue thinking about you.
Decorations of red on a green Christmas tree
Won't mean a thing if you're not here with me.
I'll have a blue Christmas, that's certain.
And when that blue heartache starts hurtin',
You'll be doin' alright, with your Christmas of white,
But I'll have a blue, blue Christmas.

Christmas Auld Lang Syne

When mistletoe and tinsel glow,
Paint a yuletide valentine.
Back home I go to those I know
For a Christmas auld lang syne.
And as we gather 'round the tree,
Our voices all combine
In sweet accord to thank the Lord
For a Christmas auld lang syne.

When sleigh bells ring and choirs sing
And the children's faces shine,
With each new toy we share their joy
With a Christmas auld lang syne.
We sing His praise this day of days
And pray next year this time
We'll all be near to share the cheer
Of a Christmas auld lang syne.

Christmas in Killarney

Christmas in Killarney is wonderful to see.
Listen to my story and I'll take you back with me.

The holly green, the ivy green,
The prettiest picture you've ever seen
Is Christmas in Killarney
With all of the folks at home.

It's nice to know, to kiss your beau
While cuddling under the mistletoe,
And Santa Claus, you know of course,
Is one of the boys from home.

The door is always open,
The neighbors pay a call,
And Father John, before he's gone,
Will bless the house and all.

How grand it feels to click your heels
And join in the fun of the jigs and reels.
I'm handing you no blarney,
The likes you've never known
Is Christmas in Killarney,
With all of the folks at home.

Christmas Time Is Here

Christmas time is here,
Happiness and cheer.
Fun for all that children call
Their favorite time of year.

Snowflakes in the air,
Carols everywhere.
Olden times and ancient rhymes
Of love and dreams to share.

Sleighbells in the air,
Beauty everywhere.
Yuletide by the fireside
And joyful memories there.
Christmas time is here,
We'll be drawing near.
Oh, that we could always see
Such spirit through the year.

The Christmas Waltz

Frosted window panes,
Candles gleaming inside,
Painted candy canes on the tree;
Santa's on his way,
He's filled his sleigh with things,
Things for you and for me.

It's that time of year,
When the world falls in love,
Every song you hear seems to say:
"Merry Christmas,
May your New Year dreams come true."
And this song of mine,
In three-quarter time,
Wishes you and yours
The same thing too.

Feliz Navidad

Feliz Navidad.
Feliz Navidad.
Feliz Navidad.
Próspero año y felicidad.

Feliz Navidad.
Feliz Navidad.
Feliz Navidad.
Próspero año y felicidad.

I want to wish you a Merry Christmas,
With lots of presents to make you happy.
I want to wish you a Merry Christmas
From the bottom of my heart.

I want to wish you a Merry Christmas,
With mistletoe and lots of cheer,
With lots of laughter throughout the years,
From the bottom of my heart.

Feliz Navidad.
Feliz Navidad.
Feliz Navidad.
Próspero año y felicidad.

Have Yourself a Merry Little Christmas

When the steeple bells sound their "A,"
They don't play it in tune.
But the welkin will ring one day,
And that day will be soon.

Have yourself a merry little Christmas,
Let your heart be light.
From now on our troubles will be out of sight.
Have yourself a merry little Christmas,
Make the Yuletide gay.
From now on our troubles will be miles away.
Here we are as in olden days,
Happy golden days of yore.
Faithful friends who are dear to us
Gather near to us once more.
Through the years we all will be together
If the fates allow.
Hang a shining star upon the highest bough,
And have yourself a merry little Christmas now.

Here we are as in olden days,
Happy golden days of yore.
Faithful friends who are dear to us
Gather near to us once more.
Through the years we all will be together
If the fates allow.
Hang a shining star upon the highest bough,
And have yourself a merry little Christmas now.

It's Beginning to Look Like Christmas

It's beginning to look a lot like Christmas,
Everywhere you go.
Take a look in the five and ten,
Glistening once again,
With candy canes and silver lanes aglow.

It's beginning to look a lot like Christmas,
Toys in every store.
But the prettiest sight to see
Is the holly that will be
On your own front door.

A pair of hopalong boots
And a pistol that shoots
Is the wish of Barney and Ben.
Dolls that will talk
And will go for a walk
Is the hope of Janice and Jen;
And Mom and Dad can hardly wait
For school to start again.

It's beginning to look a lot like Christmas,
Everywhere you go.
There's a tree in the grand hotel,
One in the park as well,
The sturdy kind that doesn't mind a snow.

It's beginning to look a lot like Christmas,
Soon the bells will start.
And the thing that will make them ring
Is the carol that you sing
Right within your heart.

The Little Drummer Boy

Come, they told me, pa rum pum pum pum.
Our newborn King to see, pa rum pum pum pum.
Our finest gifts we bring, pa rum pum pum pum,
To lay before the King, pa rum pum pum pum,
Rum pum pum pum, rum pum pum pum.
So to honor Him, pa rum pum pum pum,
When we come.

Baby Jesu, pa rum pum pum pum.
I am a poor boy, too, pa rum pum pum pum.
I have no gift to bring, pa rum pum pum pum,
That's fit to give our King, pa rum pum pum pum,
Rum pum pum pum, rum pum pum pum.
Shall I play for you, pa rum pum pum pum,
On my drum?

Mary nodded, pa rum pum pum pum.
The ox and lamb kept time, pa rum pum pum pum.
I played my drum for Him, pa rum pum pum pum.
I played my best for Him, pa rum pum pum pum,
Rum pum pum pum, rum pum pum pum.
Then He smiled at me, pa rum pum pum pum,
Me and my drum.

Little Saint Nick

Ooh, Merry Christmas, Saint Nick. Ooh.
(Christmas comes this time each year.)

Well, way up north where the air gets cold,
There's a tale about Christmas that you've
    all been told.
And a real famous cat all dressed up in red,
And he spends the whole year workin' out
    on his sled.

It's the Little Saint Nick. (Little Saint Nick.)
It's the Little Saint Nick. (Little Saint Nick.)

Just a little bobsled, we call it Old Saint Nick,
But she'll walk a toboggan with a four-speed stick.
She's candy-apple red with a ski for a wheel,
And when Santa hits the gas, man, just watch
    her peel.

It's the Little Saint Nick. (Little Saint Nick.)
It's the Little Saint Nick. (Little Saint Nick.)

❄ ❄ ❄ ❄ ❄ ❄ ❄ ❄ ❄ ❄ ❄

Lyrics for
Sing-A-Long Best of Christmas

All I Want for Christmas Is My Two Front Teeth

Everybody stops and stares at me.
These two teeth are gone, as you can see.
I don't know just who to blame for this catastrophe!
But my one wish for Christmas Eve is as plain as
  it can be!

All I want for Christmas is my two front teeth,
My two front teeth, see, my two front teeth!
Gee, if I could only have my two front teeth,
Then I could wish you, "Merry Christmas!"

It seems so long since I could say,
"Sister Susie sitting on a thistle!"
Gosh, oh gee, how happy I'd be,
If I could only whistle.

All I want for Christmas is my two front teeth,
My two front teeth, see, my two front teeth!
Gee, if I could only have my two front teeth,
Then I could wish you, "Merry Christmas!"

Blue Christmas

I'll have a blue Christmas, without you.
I'll be so blue thinking about you.
Decorations of red on a green Christmas tree
Won't mean a thing if you're not here with me.
I'll have a blue Christmas, that's certain.
And when that blue heartache starts hurtin',
You'll be doin' alright, with your Christmas of white,
But I'll have a blue, blue Christmas.

Christmas Auld Lang Syne

When mistletoe and tinsel glow,
Paint a yuletide valentine.
Back home I go to those I know
For a Christmas auld lang syne.
And as we gather 'round the tree,
Our voices all combine
In sweet accord to thank the Lord
For a Christmas auld lang syne.

When sleigh bells ring and choirs sing
And the children's faces shine,
With each new toy we share their joy
With a Christmas auld lang syne.
We sing His praise this day of days
And pray next year this time
We'll all be near to share the cheer
Of a Christmas auld lang syne.

Christmas in Killarney

Christmas in Killarney is wonderful to see.
Listen to my story and I'll take you back with me.

The holly green, the ivy green,
The prettiest picture you've ever seen
Is Christmas in Killarney
With all of the folks at home.

It's nice to know, to kiss your beau
While cuddling under the mistletoe,
And Santa Claus, you know of course,
Is one of the boys from home.

The door is always open,
The neighbors pay a call,
And Father John, before he's gone,
Will bless the house and all.

How grand it feels to click your heels
And join in the fun of the jigs and reels.
I'm handing you no blarney,
The likes you've never known
Is Christmas in Killarney,
With all of the folks at home.

Christmas Time Is Here

Christmas time is here,
Happiness and cheer.
Fun for all that children call
Their favorite time of year.

Snowflakes in the air,
Carols everywhere.
Olden times and ancient rhymes
Of love and dreams to share.

Sleighbells in the air,
Beauty everywhere.
Yuletide by the fireside
And joyful memories there.
Christmas time is here,
We'll be drawing near.
Oh, that we could always see
Such spirit through the year.

The Christmas Waltz

Frosted window panes,
Candles gleaming inside,
Painted candy canes on the tree;
Santa's on his way,
He's filled his sleigh with things,
Things for you and for me.

It's that time of year,
When the world falls in love,
Every song you hear seems to say:
"Merry Christmas,
May your New Year dreams come true."
And this song of mine,
In three-quarter time,
Wishes you and yours
The same thing too.

Feliz Navidad

Feliz Navidad.
Feliz Navidad.
Feliz Navidad.
Próspero año y felicidad.

Feliz Navidad.
Feliz Navidad.
Feliz Navidad.
Próspero año y felicidad.

I want to wish you a Merry Christmas,
With lots of presents to make you happy.
I want to wish you a Merry Christmas
From the bottom of my heart.

I want to wish you a Merry Christmas,
With mistletoe and lots of cheer,
With lots of laughter throughout the years,
From the bottom of my heart.

Feliz Navidad.
Feliz Navidad.
Feliz Navidad.
Próspero año y felicidad.

Have Yourself a Merry Little Christmas

When the steeple bells sound their "A,"
They don't play it in tune.
But the welkin will ring one day,
And that day will be soon.

Have yourself a merry little Christmas,
Let your heart be light.
From now on our troubles will be out of sight.
Have yourself a merry little Christmas,
Make the Yuletide gay.
From now on our troubles will be miles away.
Here we are as in olden days,
Happy golden days of yore.
Faithful friends who are dear to us
Gather near to us once more.
Through the years we all will be together
If the fates allow.
Hang a shining star upon the highest bough,
And have yourself a merry little Christmas now.

Here we are as in olden days,
Happy golden days of yore.
Faithful friends who are dear to us
Gather near to us once more.
Through the years we all will be together
If the fates allow.
Hang a shining star upon the highest bough,
And have yourself a merry little Christmas now.

It's Beginning to Look Like Christmas

It's beginning to look a lot like Christmas,
Everywhere you go.
Take a look in the five and ten,
Glistening once again,
With candy canes and silver lanes aglow.

It's beginning to look a lot like Christmas,
Toys in every store.
But the prettiest sight to see
Is the holly that will be
On your own front door.

A pair of hopalong boots
And a pistol that shoots
Is the wish of Barney and Ben.
Dolls that will talk
And will go for a walk
Is the hope of Janice and Jen;
And Mom and Dad can hardly wait
For school to start again.

It's beginning to look a lot like Christmas,
Everywhere you go.
There's a tree in the grand hotel,
One in the park as well,
The sturdy kind that doesn't mind a snow.

It's beginning to look a lot like Christmas,
Soon the bells will start.
And the thing that will make them ring
Is the carol that you sing
Right within your heart.

The Little Drummer Boy

Come, they told me, pa rum pum pum pum.
Our newborn King to see, pa rum pum pum pum.
Our finest gifts we bring, pa rum pum pum pum,
To lay before the King, pa rum pum pum pum,
Rum pum pum pum, rum pum pum pum.
So to honor Him, pa rum pum pum pum,
When we come.

Baby Jesu, pa rum pum pum pum.
I am a poor boy, too, pa rum pum pum pum.
I have no gift to bring, pa rum pum pum pum,
That's fit to give our King, pa rum pum pum pum,
Rum pum pum pum, rum pum pum pum.
Shall I play for you, pa rum pum pum pum,
On my drum?

Mary nodded, pa rum pum pum pum.
The ox and lamb kept time, pa rum pum pum pum.
I played my drum for Him, pa rum pum pum pum.
I played my best for Him, pa rum pum pum pum,
Rum pum pum pum, rum pum pum pum.
Then He smiled at me, pa rum pum pum pum,
Me and my drum.

Little Saint Nick

Ooh, Merry Christmas, Saint Nick. Ooh.
(Christmas comes this time each year.)

Well, way up north where the air gets cold,
There's a tale about Christmas that you've
    all been told.
And a real famous cat all dressed up in red,
And he spends the whole year workin' out
    on his sled.

It's the Little Saint Nick. (Little Saint Nick.)
It's the Little Saint Nick. (Little Saint Nick.)

Just a little bobsled, we call it Old Saint Nick,
But she'll walk a toboggan with a four-speed stick.
She's candy-apple red with a ski for a wheel,
And when Santa hits the gas, man, just watch
    her peel.

It's the Little Saint Nick. (Little Saint Nick.)
It's the Little Saint Nick. (Little Saint Nick.)

Lyrics for
Sing-A-Long Best of Christmas

❄ ❄ ❄ ❄ ❄ ❄ ❄ ❄ ❄ ❄ ❄ ❄

All I Want for Christmas Is My Two Front Teeth

Everybody stops and stares at me.
These two teeth are gone, as you can see.
I don't know just who to blame for this catastrophe!
But my one wish for Christmas Eve is as plain as
 it can be!

All I want for Christmas is my two front teeth,
My two front teeth, see, my two front teeth!
Gee, if I could only have my two front teeth,
Then I could wish you, "Merry Christmas!"

It seems so long since I could say,
"Sister Susie sitting on a thistle!"
Gosh, oh gee, how happy I'd be,
If I could only whistle.

All I want for Christmas is my two front teeth,
My two front teeth, see, my two front teeth!
Gee, if I could only have my two front teeth,
Then I could wish you, "Merry Christmas!"

Blue Christmas

I'll have a blue Christmas, without you.
I'll be so blue thinking about you.
Decorations of red on a green Christmas tree
Won't mean a thing if you're not here with me.
I'll have a blue Christmas, that's certain.
And when that blue heartache starts hurtin',
You'll be doin' alright, with your Christmas of white,
But I'll have a blue, blue Christmas.

Christmas Auld Lang Syne

When mistletoe and tinsel glow,
Paint a yuletide valentine.
Back home I go to those I know
For a Christmas auld lang syne.
And as we gather 'round the tree,
Our voices all combine
In sweet accord to thank the Lord
For a Christmas auld lang syne.

When sleigh bells ring and choirs sing
And the children's faces shine,
With each new toy we share their joy
With a Christmas auld lang syne.
We sing His praise this day of days
And pray next year this time
We'll all be near to share the cheer
Of a Christmas auld lang syne.

Christmas in Killarney

Christmas in Killarney is wonderful to see.
Listen to my story and I'll take you back with me.

The holly green, the ivy green,
The prettiest picture you've ever seen
Is Christmas in Killarney
With all of the folks at home.

It's nice to know, to kiss your beau
While cuddling under the mistletoe,
And Santa Claus, you know of course,
Is one of the boys from home.

The door is always open,
The neighbors pay a call,
And Father John, before he's gone,
Will bless the house and all.

How grand it feels to click your heels
And join in the fun of the jigs and reels.
I'm handing you no blarney,
The likes you've never known
Is Christmas in Killarney,
With all of the folks at home.

Christmas Time Is Here

Christmas time is here,
Happiness and cheer.
Fun for all that children call
Their favorite time of year.

Snowflakes in the air,
Carols everywhere.
Olden times and ancient rhymes
Of love and dreams to share.

Sleighbells in the air,
Beauty everywhere.
Yuletide by the fireside
And joyful memories there.
Christmas time is here,
We'll be drawing near.
Oh, that we could always see
Such spirit through the year.

The Christmas Waltz

Frosted window panes,
Candles gleaming inside,
Painted candy canes on the tree;
Santa's on his way,
He's filled his sleigh with things,
Things for you and for me.

It's that time of year,
When the world falls in love,
Every song you hear seems to say:
"Merry Christmas,
May your New Year dreams come true."
And this song of mine,
In three-quarter time,
Wishes you and yours
The same thing too.

❄ ❄ ❄ ❄ ❄ ❄ ❄ ❄ ❄ ❄ ❄ ❄

Feliz Navidad

Feliz Navidad.
Feliz Navidad.
Feliz Navidad.
Próspero año y felicidad.

Feliz Navidad.
Feliz Navidad.
Feliz Navidad.
Próspero año y felicidad.

I want to wish you a Merry Christmas,
With lots of presents to make you happy.
I want to wish you a Merry Christmas
From the bottom of my heart.

I want to wish you a Merry Christmas,
With mistletoe and lots of cheer,
With lots of laughter throughout the years,
From the bottom of my heart.

Feliz Navidad.
Feliz Navidad.
Feliz Navidad.
Próspero año y felicidad.

Have Yourself a Merry Little Christmas

When the steeple bells sound their "A,"
They don't play it in tune.
But the welkin will ring one day,
And that day will be soon.

Have yourself a merry little Christmas,
Let your heart be light.
From now on our troubles will be out of sight.
Have yourself a merry little Christmas,
Make the Yuletide gay.
From now on our troubles will be miles away.
Here we are as in olden days,
Happy golden days of yore.
Faithful friends who are dear to us
Gather near to us once more.
Through the years we all will be together
If the fates allow.
Hang a shining star upon the highest bough,
And have yourself a merry little Christmas now.

Here we are as in olden days,
Happy golden days of yore.
Faithful friends who are dear to us
Gather near to us once more.
Through the years we all will be together
If the fates allow.
Hang a shining star upon the highest bough,
And have yourself a merry little Christmas now.

It's Beginning to Look Like Christmas

It's beginning to look a lot like Christmas,
Everywhere you go.
Take a look in the five and ten,
Glistening once again,
With candy canes and silver lanes aglow.

It's beginning to look a lot like Christmas,
Toys in every store.
But the prettiest sight to see
Is the holly that will be
On your own front door.

A pair of hopalong boots
And a pistol that shoots
Is the wish of Barney and Ben.
Dolls that will talk
And will go for a walk
Is the hope of Janice and Jen;
And Mom and Dad can hardly wait
For school to start again.

It's beginning to look a lot like Christmas,
Everywhere you go.
There's a tree in the grand hotel,
One in the park as well,
The sturdy kind that doesn't mind a snow.

It's beginning to look a lot like Christmas,
Soon the bells will start.
And the thing that will make them ring
Is the carol that you sing
Right within your heart.

The Little Drummer Boy

Come, they told me, pa rum pum pum pum.
Our newborn King to see, pa rum pum pum pum.
Our finest gifts we bring, pa rum pum pum pum,
To lay before the King, pa rum pum pum pum,
Rum pum pum pum, rum pum pum pum.
So to honor Him, pa rum pum pum pum,
When we come.

Baby Jesu, pa rum pum pum pum.
I am a poor boy, too, pa rum pum pum pum.
I have no gift to bring, pa rum pum pum pum,
That's fit to give our King, pa rum pum pum pum,
Rum pum pum pum, rum pum pum pum.
Shall I play for you, pa rum pum pum pum,
On my drum?

Mary nodded, pa rum pum pum pum.
The ox and lamb kept time, pa rum pum pum pum.
I played my drum for Him, pa rum pum pum pum.
I played my best for Him, pa rum pum pum pum,
Rum pum pum pum, rum pum pum pum.
Then He smiled at me, pa rum pum pum pum,
Me and my drum.

Little Saint Nick

Ooh, Merry Christmas, Saint Nick. Ooh.
(Christmas comes this time each year.)

Well, way up north where the air gets cold,
There's a tale about Christmas that you've
all been told.
And a real famous cat all dressed up in red,
And he spends the whole year workin' out
on his sled.

It's the Little Saint Nick. (Little Saint Nick.)
It's the Little Saint Nick. (Little Saint Nick.)

Just a little bobsled, we call it Old Saint Nick,
But she'll walk a toboggan with a four-speed stick.
She's candy-apple red with a ski for a wheel,
And when Santa hits the gas, man, just watch
her peel.

It's the Little Saint Nick. (Little Saint Nick.)
It's the Little Saint Nick. (Little Saint Nick.)

❄ ❄ ❄ ❄ ❄ ❄ ❄ ❄ ❄ ❄ ❄

Lyrics for
Sing-A-Long Best of Christmas

All I Want for Christmas Is My Two Front Teeth

Everybody stops and stares at me.
These two teeth are gone, as you can see.
I don't know just who to blame for this catastrophe!
But my one wish for Christmas Eve is as plain as
 it can be!

All I want for Christmas is my two front teeth,
My two front teeth, see, my two front teeth!
Gee, if I could only have my two front teeth,
Then I could wish you, "Merry Christmas!"

It seems so long since I could say,
"Sister Susie sitting on a thistle!"
Gosh, oh gee, how happy I'd be,
If I could only whistle.

All I want for Christmas is my two front teeth,
My two front teeth, see, my two front teeth!
Gee, if I could only have my two front teeth,
Then I could wish you, "Merry Christmas!"

Blue Christmas

I'll have a blue Christmas, without you.
I'll be so blue thinking about you.
Decorations of red on a green Christmas tree
Won't mean a thing if you're not here with me.
I'll have a blue Christmas, that's certain.
And when that blue heartache starts hurtin',
You'll be doin' alright, with your Christmas of white,
But I'll have a blue, blue Christmas.

Christmas Auld Lang Syne

When mistletoe and tinsel glow,
Paint a yuletide valentine.
Back home I go to those I know
For a Christmas auld lang syne.
And as we gather 'round the tree,
Our voices all combine
In sweet accord to thank the Lord
For a Christmas auld lang syne.

When sleigh bells ring and choirs sing
And the children's faces shine,
With each new toy we share their joy
With a Christmas auld lang syne.
We sing His praise this day of days
And pray next year this time
We'll all be near to share the cheer
Of a Christmas auld lang syne.

Christmas in Killarney

Christmas in Killarney is wonderful to see.
Listen to my story and I'll take you back with me.

The holly green, the ivy green,
The prettiest picture you've ever seen
Is Christmas in Killarney
With all of the folks at home.

It's nice to know, to kiss your beau
While cuddling under the mistletoe,
And Santa Claus, you know of course,
Is one of the boys from home.

The door is always open,
The neighbors pay a call,
And Father John, before he's gone,
Will bless the house and all.

How grand it feels to click your heels
And join in the fun of the jigs and reels.
I'm handing you no blarney,
The likes you've never known
Is Christmas in Killarney,
With all of the folks at home.

Christmas Time Is Here

Christmas time is here,
Happiness and cheer.
Fun for all that children call
Their favorite time of year.

Snowflakes in the air,
Carols everywhere.
Olden times and ancient rhymes
Of love and dreams to share.

Sleighbells in the air,
Beauty everywhere.
Yuletide by the fireside
And joyful memories there.
Christmas time is here,
We'll be drawing near.
Oh, that we could always see
Such spirit through the year.

The Christmas Waltz

Frosted window panes,
Candles gleaming inside,
Painted candy canes on the tree;
Santa's on his way,
He's filled his sleigh with things,
Things for you and for me.

It's that time of year,
When the world falls in love,
Every song you hear seems to say:
"Merry Christmas,
May your New Year dreams come true."
And this song of mine,
In three-quarter time,
Wishes you and yours
The same thing too.

Feliz Navidad

Feliz Navidad.
Feliz Navidad.
Feliz Navidad.
Próspero año y felicidad.

Feliz Navidad.
Feliz Navidad.
Feliz Navidad.
Próspero año y felicidad.

I want to wish you a Merry Christmas,
With lots of presents to make you happy.
I want to wish you a Merry Christmas
From the bottom of my heart.

I want to wish you a Merry Christmas,
With mistletoe and lots of cheer,
With lots of laughter throughout the years,
From the bottom of my heart.

Feliz Navidad.
Feliz Navidad.
Feliz Navidad.
Próspero año y felicidad.

Have Yourself a Merry Little Christmas

When the steeple bells sound their "A,"
They don't play it in tune.
But the welkin will ring one day,
And that day will be soon.

Have yourself a merry little Christmas,
Let your heart be light.
From now on our troubles will be out of sight.
Have yourself a merry little Christmas,
Make the Yuletide gay.
From now on our troubles will be miles away.
Here we are as in olden days,
Happy golden days of yore.
Faithful friends who are dear to us
Gather near to us once more.
Through the years we all will be together
If the fates allow.
Hang a shining star upon the highest bough,
And have yourself a merry little Christmas now.

Here we are as in olden days,
Happy golden days of yore.
Faithful friends who are dear to us
Gather near to us once more.
Through the years we all will be together
If the fates allow.
Hang a shining star upon the highest bough,
And have yourself a merry little Christmas now.

It's Beginning to Look Like Christmas

It's beginning to look a lot like Christmas,
Everywhere you go.
Take a look in the five and ten,
Glistening once again,
With candy canes and silver lanes aglow.

It's beginning to look a lot like Christmas,
Toys in every store.
But the prettiest sight to see
Is the holly that will be
On your own front door.

A pair of hopalong boots
And a pistol that shoots
Is the wish of Barney and Ben.
Dolls that will talk
And will go for a walk
Is the hope of Janice and Jen;
And Mom and Dad can hardly wait
For school to start again.

It's beginning to look a lot like Christmas,
Everywhere you go.
There's a tree in the grand hotel,
One in the park as well,
The sturdy kind that doesn't mind a snow.

It's beginning to look a lot like Christmas,
Soon the bells will start.
And the thing that will make them ring
Is the carol that you sing
Right within your heart.

The Little Drummer Boy

Come, they told me, pa rum pum pum pum.
Our newborn King to see, pa rum pum pum pum.
Our finest gifts we bring, pa rum pum pum pum,
To lay before the King, pa rum pum pum pum,
Rum pum pum pum, rum pum pum pum.
So to honor Him, pa rum pum pum pum,
When we come.

Baby Jesu, pa rum pum pum pum.
I am a poor boy, too, pa rum pum pum pum.
I have no gift to bring, pa rum pum pum pum,
That's fit to give our King, pa rum pum pum pum,
Rum pum pum pum, rum pum pum pum.
Shall I play for you, pa rum pum pum pum,
On my drum?

Mary nodded, pa rum pum pum pum.
The ox and lamb kept time, pa rum pum pum pum.
I played my drum for Him, pa rum pum pum pum.
I played my best for Him, pa rum pum pum pum,
Rum pum pum pum, rum pum pum pum.
Then He smiled at me, pa rum pum pum pum,
Me and my drum.

Little Saint Nick

Ooh, Merry Christmas, Saint Nick. Ooh.
(Christmas comes this time each year.)

Well, way up north where the air gets cold,
There's a tale about Christmas that you've
all been told.
And a real famous cat all dressed up in red,
And he spends the whole year workin' out
on his sled.

It's the Little Saint Nick. (Little Saint Nick.)
It's the Little Saint Nick. (Little Saint Nick.)

Just a little bobsled, we call it Old Saint Nick,
But she'll walk a toboggan with a four-speed stick.
She's candy-apple red with a ski for a wheel,
And when Santa hits the gas, man, just watch
her peel.

It's the Little Saint Nick. (Little Saint Nick.)
It's the Little Saint Nick. (Little Saint Nick.)

Run, run, reindeer.
Run, run, reindeer.
Oh, run, run, reindeer.
Run, run, reindeer.
He don't miss no one.

And haulin' through the snow at a fright'nin' speed
With a half a dozen deer with Rudy to lead.
He's gotta wear his goggles 'cause the snow
   really flies,
And he's cruisin' every pad with a little surprise.

It's the Little Saint Nick. (Little Saint Nick.)
It's the Little Saint Nick. (Little Saint Nick.)

Ah, Merry Christmas, Saint Nick.
(Christmas comes this time each year.)

A Marshmallow World

It's a marshmallow world in the winter
When the snow comes to cover the ground.
It's the time for play. It's a whipped-cream day.
I wait for it the whole year 'round.

Those are marshmallow clouds being friendly
In the arms of the evergreen trees.
And the sun is red like a pumpkin head.
It's shining so your nose won't freeze.

The world is your snowball, see how it grows.
That's how it goes, whenever it snows.
The world is your snowball, just for a song.
Get out and roll it along.

It's a yum, yummy world made for sweethearts.
Take a walk with your favorite girl.
It's a sugar date, what if spring is late?
In winter it's a marshmallow world.

The Most Wonderful Time of the Year

It's the most wonderful time of the year,
With the kids jingle-belling and everyone
   telling you,
"Be of good cheer."
It's the most wonderful time of the year.

It's the hap-happiest season of all,
With those holiday greetings and gay
   happy meetings,
When friends come to call.
It's the hap-happiest season of all.

There'll be parties for hosting,
Marshmallows for toasting,
And caroling out in the snow.
There'll be scary ghost stories
And tales of the glories
Of Christmases long, long ago.

It's the most wonderful time of the year.
There'll be much mistltoe-ing, and hearts will
   be glowing
When loved ones are near.
It's the most wonderful time of the year.

It's the most wonderful time of the year.
There'll be much mistltoe-ing, and hearts will
   be glowing
When loved ones are near.
It's the most wonderful time,
It's the most wonderful time,
It's the most wonderful time of the year.

Sleigh Ride

Just hear those sleigh bells jingling,
Ring-ting-tingling, too.
Come on, it's lovely weather
For a sleigh ride together with you.
Outside, the snow is falling,
And friends are calling, "Yoo hoo."
Come on, it's lovely weather
For a sleigh ride together with you.

Giddy-yap, giddy-yap, giddy-yap, let's go!
Let's look at the show.
We're riding in a wonderland of snow.
Giddy-yap, giddy-yap, giddy-yap, it's grand
Just holding your hand.
We're gliding along with the song
Of a wintery fairyland.

Our cheeks are nice and rosy,
And comfy cozy are we.
We're snuggled up together
Like two birds of a feather would be.
Let's take that road before us
And sing a chorus or two.
Come on, it's lovely weather
For a sleigh ride together with you. ❄

There's a birthday party at the home of
   Farmer Gray.
It'll be the perfect ending of a perfect day.
We'll be singing the songs we love to sing
   without a single stop
At the fireplace, while we watch the chestnuts pop.
Pop! Pop! Pop!

There's a happy feeling nothing in the world
   can buy,
When they pass around the coffee and the
   pumpkin pie.
It'll nearly be like a picture print by Currier
   and Ives.
These wonderful things are the things we
   remember all through our lives.

Just hear...
(repeat from beginning to snowflake)

Snowfall

Snowfall, softly, gently drift down.
Snowflakes whisper 'neath my window.
Covering trees misty white,
Velvet breeze 'round my doorstep.
Gently, softly, silent snowfall!

❄ ❄ ❄ ❄ ❄ ❄ ❄ ❄ ❄ ❄ ❄

We Need a Little Christmas

Haul out the holly,
Put up the tree before my
Spirit falls again.
Fill up the stocking,
I may be rushing things, but
Deck the halls again now.

For we need a little Christmas,
Right this very minute,
Candles in the window,
Carols at the spinet.
Yes, we need a little Christmas,
Right this very minute,
It hasn't snowed a single flurry,
But Santa, dear, we're in a hurry.

So climb down the chimney,
Turn on the brightest string of
Lights I've ever seen,
Slice up the fruitcake,
It's time we hung some tinsel
On that evergreen bough.

For I've grown a little leaner,
Grown a little colder,
Grown a little sadder,
Grown a little older.
And I need a little angel,
Sitting on my shoulder,
I need a little Christmas now!

For we need a little music,
Need a little laughter,
Need a little singing
Ringing through the rafter.
And we need a little snappy
"Happy ever after,"
We need a little Christmas now!

Music and Lyric by Jerry Herman
© 1966 (Renewed) JERRY HERMAN
All Rights Controlled by JERRYCO MUSIC CO.
Exclusive Agent: EDWIN H. MORRIS & COMPANY, A Division of MPL Music
Publishing, Inc.

White Christmas

The sun is shining, the grass is green,
The orange and palm trees sway.
There's never been such a day
In Beverly Hills, L. A.
But it's December the twenty-fourth,
And I am longing to be up north.

I'm dreaming of a white Christmas,
Just like the ones I used to know,
Where the treetops glisten and children listen
To hear sleigh bells in the snow.

I'm dreaming of a white Christmas
With every Christmas card I write:
"May your days be merry and bright
And may all your Christmases be white."

Words and Music by Irving Berlin
© Copyright 1940, 1942 by Irving Berlin
Copyright Renewed

Winter Wonderland

Over the ground lies a mantle of white,
A heaven of diamonds shine down through the night;
Two hearts are thillin' in spite of the chill in the
    weather.

Love knows no season; love knows no clime;
Romance can blossom any old time.
Here in the open, we're walkin' and hopin' together!

Sleigh bells ring, are you list'nin'?
In the lane, snow is glist'nin'.
A beautiful sight, we're happy tonight,
Walkin' in a winter wonderland.
Gone away is the bluebird,
Here to stay is the new bird.
He sings a love song as we go along,
Walkin' in a winter wonderland!

In the meadow we can build a snowman,
And pretend that he is Parson Brown.
He'll say, "Are you married?" We'll say, "No, man!
But you can do the job when you're in town!"
Later on, we'll conspire, as we dream by the fire,
To face unafraid the plans that we made,
Walkin' in a winter wonderland!

Sleigh bells ring, are you list'nin'?
In the lane, snow is glist'nin'.
A beautiful sight, we're happy tonight,
Walkin' in a winter wonderland.
Gone away is the bluebird,
Here to stay is the new bird.
He's singing a song as we go along,
Walkin' in a winter wonderland!

In the meadow we can build a snowman,
And pretend that he's a circus clown.
We'll have lots of fun with Mister Snowman,
Until the other kiddies knock him down!
When it snows, ain't it thrillin',
Though your nose gets a chillin'?
We'll frolic and play the Eskimo way,
Walkin' in a winter wonderland!

Words by Dick Smith
Music by Felix Bernard
© 1934 (Renewed) WB MUSIC CORP.
All Rights in Canada Administered by REDWOOD MUSIC LTD.

Wonderful Christmastime

The mood is right, the spirit's up,
We're here tonight and that's enough.
Simply having a wonderful Christmastime.
Simply having a wonderful Christmastime.

The party's on, the feeling's here
That only comes this time of year.
Simply having a wonderful Christmastime.
Simply having a wonderful Christmastime.

The choir of children sing their song.
Ding dong, ding dong.
Ding dong ding.
Ooh, ooh.
Do do do do do do do.

We're simply having a wonderful Christmastime.
Simply having a wonderful Christmastime.

The word is out about the town,
To lift a glass, oh, don't look down.
Simply having a wonderful Christmastime.
Simply having a wonderful Christmastime.

The choir of children sing their song.
(They practiced all year long.)
Ding dong, ding dong, ding dong,
Ding dong, ding dong, ding dong,
Dong, dong, dong, dong.

The party's on, the spirit's up.
We're here tonight and that's enough.
Simply having a wonderful Christmastime.
We're simply having a wonderful Christmastime.

Words and Music by Paul McCartney
© 1979 MPL COMMUNICATIONS LTD.
Administered by MPL COMMUNICATIONS, INC.

You're All I Want for Christmas

When Santa comes around at Christmas time
And leaves a lot of cheer at every door,
If he would only grant the wish in my heart
I would never ask for more.

You're all I want for Christmas,
All I want my whole life through.
Each day is just like Christmas
Any time that I'm with you.

You're all I want for Christmas,
And if all my dreams come true,
Then I'll awake on Christmas morning
And find my stocking filled with you.

Words and Music by Glen Moore and Seger Ellis
Copyright © 1948 SONGS OF UNIVERSAL, INC.
Copyright Renewed

Run, run, reindeer.
Run, run, reindeer.
Oh, run, run, reindeer.
Run, run, reindeer.
He don't miss no one.

And haulin' through the snow at a fright'nin' speed
With a half a dozen deer with Rudy to lead.
He's gotta wear his goggles 'cause the snow
  really flies,
And he's cruisin' every pad with a little surprise.

It's the Little Saint Nick. (Little Saint Nick.)
It's the Little Saint Nick. (Little Saint Nick.)

Ah, Merry Christmas, Saint Nick.
(Christmas comes this time each year.)

A Marshmallow World

It's a marshmallow world in the winter
When the snow comes to cover the ground.
It's the time for play. It's a whipped-cream day.
I wait for it the whole year 'round.

Those are marshmallow clouds being friendly
In the arms of the evergreen trees.
And the sun is red like a pumpkin head.
It's shining so your nose won't freeze.

The world is your snowball, see how it grows.
That's how it goes, whenever it snows.
The world is your snowball, just for a song.
Get out and roll it along.

It's a yum, yummy world made for sweethearts.
Take a walk with your favorite girl.
It's a sugar date, what if spring is late?
In winter it's a marshmallow world.

The Most Wonderful Time of the Year

It's the most wonderful time of the year,
With the kids jingle-belling and everyone
  telling you,
"Be of good cheer."
It's the most wonderful time of the year.

It's the hap-happiest season of all,
With those holiday greetings and gay
  happy meetings,
When friends come to call.
It's the hap-happiest season of all.

There'll be parties for hosting,
Marshmallows for toasting,
And caroling out in the snow.
There'll be scary ghost stories
And tales of the glories
Of Christmases long, long ago.

It's the most wonderful time of the year.
There'll be much mistltoe-ing, and hearts will
  be glowing
When loved ones are near.
It's the most wonderful time of the year.

It's the most wonderful time of the year.
There'll be much mistltoe-ing, and hearts will
  be glowing
When loved ones are near.
It's the most wonderful time,
It's the most wonderful time,
It's the most wonderful time of the year.

Sleigh Ride

Just hear those sleigh bells jingling,
Ring-ting-tingling, too.
Come on, it's lovely weather
For a sleigh ride together with you.
Outside, the snow is falling,
And friends are calling, "Yoo hoo."
Come on, it's lovely weather
For a sleigh ride together with you.

Giddy-yap, giddy-yap, giddy-yap, let's go!
Let's look at the show.
We're riding in a wonderland of snow.
Giddy-yap, giddy-yap, giddy-yap, it's grand
Just holding your hand.
We're gliding along with the song
Of a wintery fairyland.

Our cheeks are nice and rosy,
And comfy cozy are we.
We're snuggled up together
Like two birds of a feather would be.
Let's take that road before us
And sing a chorus or two.
Come on, it's lovely weather
For a sleigh ride together with you. ❊

There's a birthday party at the home of
  Farmer Gray.
It'll be the perfect ending of a perfect day.
We'll be singing the songs we love to sing
  without a single stop
At the fireplace, while we watch the chestnuts pop.
Pop! Pop! Pop!

There's a happy feeling nothing in the world
  can buy,
When they pass around the coffee and the
  pumpkin pie.
It'll nearly be like a picture print by Currier
  and Ives.
These wonderful things are the things we
  remember all through our lives.

Just hear...
(repeat from beginning to snowflake)

Snowfall

Snowfall, softly, gently drift down.
Snowflakes whisper 'neath my window.
Covering trees misty white,
Velvet breeze 'round my doorstep.
Gently, softly, silent snowfall!

❊ ❊ ❊ ❊ ❊ ❊ ❊ ❊ ❊ ❊ ❊

We Need a Little Christmas

Haul out the holly,
Put up the tree before my
Spirit falls again.
Fill up the stocking,
I may be rushing things, but
Deck the halls again now.

For we need a little Christmas,
Right this very minute,
Candles in the window,
Carols at the spinet.
Yes, we need a little Christmas,
Right this very minute,
It hasn't snowed a single flurry,
But Santa, dear, we're in a hurry.

So climb down the chimney,
Turn on the brightest string of
Lights I've ever seen,
Slice up the fruitcake,
It's time we hung some tinsel
On that evergreen bough.

For I've grown a little leaner,
Grown a little colder,
Grown a little sadder,
Grown a little older.
And I need a little angel,
Sitting on my shoulder,
I need a little Christmas now!

For we need a little music,
Need a little laughter,
Need a little singing
Ringing through the rafter.
And we need a little snappy
"Happy ever after,"
We need a little Christmas now!

White Christmas

The sun is shining, the grass is green,
The orange and palm trees sway.
There's never been such a day
In Beverly Hills, L. A.
But it's December the twenty-fourth,
And I am longing to be up north.

I'm dreaming of a white Christmas,
Just like the ones I used to know,
Where the treetops glisten and children listen
To hear sleigh bells in the snow.

I'm dreaming of a white Christmas
With every Christmas card I write:
"May your days be merry and bright
And may all your Christmases be white."

Winter Wonderland

Over the ground lies a mantle of white,
A heaven of diamonds shine down through the night;
Two hearts are thillin' in spite of the chill in the
    weather.

Love knows no season; love knows no clime;
Romance can blossom any old time.
Here in the open, we're walkin' and hopin' together!

Sleigh bells ring, are you list'nin'?
In the lane, snow is glist'nin'.
A beautiful sight, we're happy tonight,
Walkin' in a winter wonderland.
Gone away is the bluebird,
Here to stay is the new bird.
He sings a love song as we go along,
Walkin' in a winter wonderland!

In the meadow we can build a snowman,
And pretend that he is Parson Brown.
He'll say, "Are you married?" We'll say, "No, man!
But you can do the job when you're in town!"
Later on, we'll conspire, as we dream by the fire,
To face unafraid the plans that we made,
Walkin' in a winter wonderland!

Sleigh bells ring, are you list'nin'?
In the lane, snow is glist'nin'.
A beautiful sight, we're happy tonight,
Walkin' in a winter wonderland.
Gone away is the bluebird,
Here to stay is the new bird.
He's singing a song as we go along,
Walkin' in a winter wonderland!

In the meadow we can build a snowman,
And pretend that he's a circus clown.
We'll have lots of fun with Mister Snowman,
Until the other kiddies knock him down!
When it snows, ain't it thrillin',
Though your nose gets a chillin'?
We'll frolic and play the Eskimo way,
Walkin' in a winter wonderland!

Wonderful Christmastime

The mood is right, the spirit's up,
We're here tonight and that's enough.
Simply having a wonderful Christmastime.
Simply having a wonderful Christmastime.

The party's on, the feeling's here
That only comes this time of year.
Simply having a wonderful Christmastime.
Simply having a wonderful Christmastime.

The choir of children sing their song.
Ding dong, ding dong.
Ding dong ding.
Ooh, ooh.
Do do do do do do do.

We're simply having a wonderful Christmastime.
Simply having a wonderful Christmastime.

The word is out about the town,
To lift a glass, oh, don't look down.
Simply having a wonderful Christmastime.
Simply having a wonderful Christmastime.

The choir of children sing their song.
(They practiced all year long.)
Ding dong, ding dong, ding dong,
Ding dong, ding dong, ding dong,
Dong, dong, dong, dong.

The party's on, the spirit's up.
We're here tonight and that's enough.
Simply having a wonderful Christmastime.
We're simply having a wonderful Christmastime.

You're All I Want for Christmas

When Santa comes around at Christmas time
And leaves a lot of cheer at every door,
If he would only grant the wish in my heart
I would never ask for more.

You're all I want for Christmas,
All I want my whole life through.
Each day is just like Christmas
Any time that I'm with you.

You're all I want for Christmas,
And if all my dreams come true,
Then I'll awake on Christmas morning
And find my stocking filled with you.

❄ ❄ ❄ ❄ ❄ ❄ ❄ ❄ ❄ ❄ ❄

Run, run, reindeer.
Run, run, reindeer.
Oh, run, run, reindeer.
Run, run, reindeer.
He don't miss no one.

And haulin' through the snow at a fright'nin' speed
With a half a dozen deer with Rudy to lead.
He's gotta wear his goggles 'cause the snow
  really flies,
And he's cruisin' every pad with a little surprise.

It's the Little Saint Nick. (Little Saint Nick.)
It's the Little Saint Nick. (Little Saint Nick.)

Ah, Merry Christmas, Saint Nick.
(Christmas comes this time each year.)

Words and Music by Brian Wilson and Mike Love
Copyright © 1963 IRVING MUSIC, INC.
Copyright Renewed

A Marshmallow World

It's a marshmallow world in the winter
When the snow comes to cover the ground.
It's the time for play. It's a whipped-cream day.
I wait for it the whole year 'round.

Those are marshmallow clouds being friendly
In the arms of the evergreen trees.
And the sun is red like a pumpkin head.
It's shining so your nose won't freeze.

The world is your snowball, see how it grows.
That's how it goes, whenever it snows.
The world is your snowball, just for a song.
Get out and roll it along.

It's a yum, yummy world made for sweethearts.
Take a walk with your favorite girl.
It's a sugar date, what if spring is late?
In winter it's a marshmallow world.

Words by Carl Sigman
Music by Peter De Rose
Copyright © 1949, 1950 Shapiro, Bernstein & Co., Inc., New York
Copyright Renewed

The Most Wonderful Time of the Year

It's the most wonderful time of the year,
With the kids jingle-belling and everyone
  telling you,
"Be of good cheer."
It's the most wonderful time of the year.

It's the hap-happiest season of all,
With those holiday greetings and gay
  happy meetings,
When friends come to call.
It's the hap-happiest season of all.

There'll be parties for hosting,
Marshmallows for toasting,
And caroling out in the snow.
There'll be scary ghost stories
And tales of the glories
Of Christmases long, long ago.

It's the most wonderful time of the year.
There'll be much mistltoe-ing, and hearts will
  be glowing
When loved ones are near.
It's the most wonderful time of the year.

It's the most wonderful time of the year.
There'll be much mistltoe-ing, and hearts will
  be glowing
When loved ones are near.
It's the most wonderful time,
It's the most wonderful time,
It's the most wonderful time of the year.

Words and Music by Eddie Pola and George Wyle
Copyright © 1963 Barnaby Music Corp.
Copyright Renewed
Administered by Lichelle Music Company

Sleigh Ride

Just hear those sleigh bells jingling,
Ring-ting-tingling, too.
Come on, it's lovely weather
For a sleigh ride together with you.
Outside, the snow is falling,
And friends are calling, "Yoo hoo."
Come on, it's lovely weather
For a sleigh ride together with you.

Giddy-yap, giddy-yap, giddy-yap, let's go!
Let's look at the show.
We're riding in a wonderland of snow.
Giddy-yap, giddy-yap, giddy-yap, it's grand
Just holding your hand.
We're gliding along with the song
Of a wintery fairyland.

Our cheeks are nice and rosy,
And comfy cozy are we.
We're snuggled up together
Like two birds of a feather would be.
Let's take that road before us
And sing a chorus or two.
Come on, it's lovely weather
For a sleigh ride together with you. ※

There's a birthday party at the home of
  Farmer Gray.
It'll be the perfect ending of a perfect day.
We'll be singing the songs we love to sing
  without a single stop
At the fireplace, while we watch the chestnuts pop.
Pop! Pop! Pop!

There's a happy feeling nothing in the world
  can buy,
When they pass around the coffee and the
  pumpkin pie.
It'll nearly be like a picture print by Currier
  and Ives.
These wonderful things are the things we
  remember all through our lives.

Just hear...
(repeat from beginning to snowflake)

Music by Leroy Anderson
Words by Mitchell Parish
© 1948, 1950 (Copyrights Renewed) WOODBURY MUSIC COMPANY and
EMI MILLS MUSIC, INC.
Worldwide Print Rights Administered by ALFRED MUSIC

Snowfall

Snowfall, softly, gently drift down.
Snowflakes whisper 'neath my window.
Covering trees misty white,
Velvet breeze 'round my doorstep.
Gently, softly, silent snowfall!

Lyrics by Ruth Thornhill
Music by Claude Thornhill
© 1941 (Renewed) CHAPPELL & CO., INC.

※ ※ ※ ※ ※ ※ ※ ※ ※ ※ ※

We Need a Little Christmas

Haul out the holly,
Put up the tree before my
Spirit falls again.
Fill up the stocking,
I may be rushing things, but
Deck the halls again now.

For we need a little Christmas,
Right this very minute,
Candles in the window,
Carols at the spinet.
Yes, we need a little Christmas,
Right this very minute,
It hasn't snowed a single flurry,
But Santa, dear, we're in a hurry.

So climb down the chimney,
Turn on the brightest string of
Lights I've ever seen,
Slice up the fruitcake,
It's time we hung some tinsel
On that evergreen bough.

For I've grown a little leaner,
Grown a little colder,
Grown a little sadder,
Grown a little older.
And I need a little angel,
Sitting on my shoulder,
I need a little Christmas now!

For we need a little music,
Need a little laughter,
Need a little singing
Ringing through the rafter.
And we need a little snappy
"Happy ever after,"
We need a little Christmas now!

White Christmas

The sun is shining, the grass is green,
The orange and palm trees sway.
There's never been such a day
In Beverly Hills, L. A.
But it's December the twenty-fourth,
And I am longing to be up north.

I'm dreaming of a white Christmas,
Just like the ones I used to know,
Where the treetops glisten and children listen
To hear sleigh bells in the snow.

I'm dreaming of a white Christmas
With every Christmas card I write:
"May your days be merry and bright
And may all your Christmases be white."

Winter Wonderland

Over the ground lies a mantle of white,
A heaven of diamonds shine down through the night;
Two hearts are thillin' in spite of the chill in the
    weather.

Love knows no season; love knows no clime;
Romance can blossom any old time.
Here in the open, we're walkin' and hopin' together!

Sleigh bells ring, are you list'nin'?
In the lane, snow is glist'nin'.
A beautiful sight, we're happy tonight,
Walkin' in a winter wonderland.
Gone away is the bluebird,
Here to stay is the new bird.
He sings a love song as we go along,
Walkin' in a winter wonderland!

In the meadow we can build a snowman,
And pretend that he is Parson Brown.
He'll say, "Are you married?" We'll say, "No, man!
But you can do the job when you're in town!"
Later on, we'll conspire, as we dream by the fire,
To face unafraid the plans that we made,
Walkin' in a winter wonderland!

Sleigh bells ring, are you list'nin'?
In the lane, snow is glist'nin'.
A beautiful sight, we're happy tonight,
Walkin' in a winter wonderland.
Gone away is the bluebird,
Here to stay is the new bird.
He's singing a song as we go along,
Walkin' in a winter wonderland!

In the meadow we can build a snowman,
And pretend that he's a circus clown.
We'll have lots of fun with Mister Snowman,
Until the other kiddies knock him down!
When it snows, ain't it thrillin',
Though your nose gets a chillin'?
We'll frolic and play the Eskimo way,
Walkin' in a winter wonderland!

Wonderful Christmastime

The mood is right, the spirit's up,
We're here tonight and that's enough.
Simply having a wonderful Christmastime.
Simply having a wonderful Christmastime.

The party's on, the feeling's here
That only comes this time of year.
Simply having a wonderful Christmastime.
Simply having a wonderful Christmastime.

The choir of children sing their song.
Ding dong, ding dong.
Ding dong ding.
Ooh, ooh.
Do do do do do do do.

We're simply having a wonderful Christmastime.
Simply having a wonderful Christmastime.

The word is out about the town,
To lift a glass, oh, don't look down.
Simply having a wonderful Christmastime.
Simply having a wonderful Christmastime.

The choir of children sing their song.
(They practiced all year long.)
Ding dong, ding dong, ding dong,
Ding dong, ding dong, ding dong,
Dong, dong, dong, dong.

The party's on, the spirit's up.
We're here tonight and that's enough.
Simply having a wonderful Christmastime.
We're simply having a wonderful Christmastime.

You're All I Want for Christmas

When Santa comes around at Christmas time
And leaves a lot of cheer at every door,
If he would only grant the wish in my heart
I would never ask for more.

You're all I want for Christmas,
All I want my whole life through.
Each day is just like Christmas
Any time that I'm with you.

You're all I want for Christmas,
And if all my dreams come true,
Then I'll awake on Christmas morning
And find my stocking filled with you.

❄ ❄ ❄ ❄ ❄ ❄ ❄ ❄ ❄ ❄ ❄ ❄

Run, run, reindeer.
Run, run, reindeer.
Oh, run, run, reindeer.
Run, run, reindeer.
He don't miss no one.

And haulin' through the snow at a fright'nin' speed
With a half a dozen deer with Rudy to lead.
He's gotta wear his goggles 'cause the snow
 really flies,
And he's cruisin' every pad with a little surprise.

It's the Little Saint Nick. (Little Saint Nick.)
It's the Little Saint Nick. (Little Saint Nick.)

Ah, Merry Christmas, Saint Nick.
(Christmas comes this time each year.)

A Marshmallow World

It's a marshmallow world in the winter
When the snow comes to cover the ground.
It's the time for play. It's a whipped-cream day.
I wait for it the whole year 'round.

Those are marshmallow clouds being friendly
In the arms of the evergreen trees.
And the sun is red like a pumpkin head.
It's shining so your nose won't freeze.

The world is your snowball, see how it grows.
That's how it goes, whenever it snows.
The world is your snowball, just for a song.
Get out and roll it along.

It's a yum, yummy world made for sweethearts.
Take a walk with your favorite girl.
It's a sugar date, what if spring is late?
In winter it's a marshmallow world.

The Most Wonderful Time of the Year

It's the most wonderful time of the year,
With the kids jingle-belling and everyone
 telling you,
"Be of good cheer."
It's the most wonderful time of the year.

It's the hap-happiest season of all,
With those holiday greetings and gay
 happy meetings,
When friends come to call.
It's the hap-happiest season of all.

There'll be parties for hosting,
Marshmallows for toasting,
And caroling out in the snow.
There'll be scary ghost stories
And tales of the glories
Of Christmases long, long ago.

It's the most wonderful time of the year.
There'll be much mistltoe-ing, and hearts will
 be glowing
When loved ones are near.
It's the most wonderful time of the year.

It's the most wonderful time of the year.
There'll be much mistltoe-ing, and hearts will
 be glowing
When loved ones are near.
It's the most wonderful time,
It's the most wonderful time,
It's the most wonderful time of the year.

Sleigh Ride

Just hear those sleigh bells jingling,
Ring-ting-tingling, too.
Come on, it's lovely weather
For a sleigh ride together with you.
Outside, the snow is falling,
And friends are calling, "Yoo hoo."
Come on, it's lovely weather
For a sleigh ride together with you.

Giddy-yap, giddy-yap, giddy-yap, let's go!
Let's look at the show.
We're riding in a wonderland of snow.
Giddy-yap, giddy-yap, giddy-yap, it's grand
Just holding your hand.
We're gliding along with the song
Of a wintery fairyland.

Our cheeks are nice and rosy,
And comfy cozy are we.
We're snuggled up together
Like two birds of a feather would be.
Let's take that road before us
And sing a chorus or two.
Come on, it's lovely weather
For a sleigh ride together with you. ❊

There's a birthday party at the home of
 Farmer Gray.
It'll be the perfect ending of a perfect day.
We'll be singing the songs we love to sing
 without a single stop
At the fireplace, while we watch the chestnuts pop.
Pop! Pop! Pop!

There's a happy feeling nothing in the world
 can buy,
When they pass around the coffee and the
 pumpkin pie.
It'll nearly be like a picture print by Currier
 and Ives.
These wonderful things are the things we
 remember all through our lives.

Just hear...
(repeat from beginning to snowflake)

Snowfall

Snowfall, softly, gently drift down.
Snowflakes whisper 'neath my window.
Covering trees misty white,
Velvet breeze 'round my doorstep.
Gently, softly, silent snowfall!

❊ ❊ ❊ ❊ ❊ ❊ ❊ ❊ ❊ ❊ ❊

We Need a Little Christmas

Haul out the holly,
Put up the tree before my
Spirit falls again.
Fill up the stocking,
I may be rushing things, but
Deck the halls again now.

For we need a little Christmas,
Right this very minute,
Candles in the window,
Carols at the spinet.
Yes, we need a little Christmas,
Right this very minute,
It hasn't snowed a single flurry,
But Santa, dear, we're in a hurry.

So climb down the chimney,
Turn on the brightest string of
Lights I've ever seen,
Slice up the fruitcake,
It's time we hung some tinsel
On that evergreen bough.

For I've grown a little leaner,
Grown a little colder,
Grown a little sadder,
Grown a little older.
And I need a little angel,
Sitting on my shoulder,
I need a little Christmas now!

For we need a little music,
Need a little laughter,
Need a little singing
Ringing through the rafter.
And we need a little snappy
"Happy ever after,"
We need a little Christmas now!

White Christmas

The sun is shining, the grass is green,
The orange and palm trees sway.
There's never been such a day
In Beverly Hills, L. A.
But it's December the twenty-fourth,
And I am longing to be up north.

I'm dreaming of a white Christmas,
Just like the ones I used to know,
Where the treetops glisten and children listen
To hear sleigh bells in the snow.

I'm dreaming of a white Christmas
With every Christmas card I write:
"May your days be merry and bright
And may all your Christmases be white."

Winter Wonderland

Over the ground lies a mantle of white,
A heaven of diamonds shine down through the night;
Two hearts are thillin' in spite of the chill in the
  weather.

Love knows no season; love knows no clime;
Romance can blossom any old time.
Here in the open, we're walkin' and hopin' together!

Sleigh bells ring, are you list'nin'?
In the lane, snow is glist'nin'.
A beautiful sight, we're happy tonight,
Walkin' in a winter wonderland.
Gone away is the bluebird,
Here to stay is the new bird.
He sings a love song as we go along,
Walkin' in a winter wonderland!

In the meadow we can build a snowman,
And pretend that he is Parson Brown.
He'll say, "Are you married?" We'll say, "No, man!
But you can do the job when you're in town!"
Later on, we'll conspire, as we dream by the fire,
To face unafraid the plans that we made,
Walkin' in a winter wonderland!

Sleigh bells ring, are you list'nin'?
In the lane, snow is glist'nin'.
A beautiful sight, we're happy tonight,
Walkin' in a winter wonderland.
Gone away is the bluebird,
Here to stay is the new bird.
He's singing a song as we go along,
Walkin' in a winter wonderland!

In the meadow we can build a snowman,
And pretend that he's a circus clown.
We'll have lots of fun with Mister Snowman,
Until the other kiddies knock him down!
When it snows, ain't it thrillin',
Though your nose gets a chillin'?
We'll frolic and play the Eskimo way,
Walkin' in a winter wonderland!

Wonderful Christmastime

The mood is right, the spirit's up,
We're here tonight and that's enough.
Simply having a wonderful Christmastime.
Simply having a wonderful Christmastime.

The party's on, the feeling's here
That only comes this time of year.
Simply having a wonderful Christmastime.
Simply having a wonderful Christmastime.

The choir of children sing their song.
Ding dong, ding dong.
Ding dong ding.
Ooh, ooh.
Do do do do do do do.

We're simply having a wonderful Christmastime.
Simply having a wonderful Christmastime.

The word is out about the town,
To lift a glass, oh, don't look down.
Simply having a wonderful Christmastime.
Simply having a wonderful Christmastime.

The choir of children sing their song.
(They practiced all year long.)
Ding dong, ding dong, ding dong,
Ding dong, ding dong, ding dong,
Dong, dong, dong, dong.

The party's on, the spirit's up.
We're here tonight and that's enough.
Simply having a wonderful Christmastime.
We're simply having a wonderful Christmastime.

You're All I Want for Christmas

When Santa comes around at Christmas time
And leaves a lot of cheer at every door,
If he would only grant the wish in my heart
I would never ask for more.

You're all I want for Christmas,
All I want my whole life through.
Each day is just like Christmas
Any time that I'm with you.

You're all I want for Christmas,
And if all my dreams come true,
Then I'll awake on Christmas morning
And find my stocking filled with you.

❄ ❄ ❄ ❄ ❄ ❄ ❄ ❄ ❄ ❄ ❄

Run, run, reindeer.
Run, run, reindeer.
Oh, run, run, reindeer.
Run, run, reindeer.
He don't miss no one.

And haulin' through the snow at a fright'nin' speed
With a half a dozen deer with Rudy to lead.
He's gotta wear his goggles 'cause the snow
  really flies,
And he's cruisin' every pad with a little surprise.

It's the Little Saint Nick. (Little Saint Nick.)
It's the Little Saint Nick. (Little Saint Nick.)

Ah, Merry Christmas, Saint Nick.
(Christmas comes this time each year.)

A Marshmallow World

It's a marshmallow world in the winter
When the snow comes to cover the ground.
It's the time for play. It's a whipped-cream day.
I wait for it the whole year 'round.

Those are marshmallow clouds being friendly
In the arms of the evergreen trees.
And the sun is red like a pumpkin head.
It's shining so your nose won't freeze.

The world is your snowball, see how it grows.
That's how it goes, whenever it snows.
The world is your snowball, just for a song.
Get out and roll it along.

It's a yum, yummy world made for sweethearts.
Take a walk with your favorite girl.
It's a sugar date, what if spring is late?
In winter it's a marshmallow world.

The Most Wonderful Time of the Year

It's the most wonderful time of the year,
With the kids jingle-belling and everyone
  telling you,
"Be of good cheer."
It's the most wonderful time of the year.

It's the hap-happiest season of all,
With those holiday greetings and gay
  happy meetings,
When friends come to call.
It's the hap-happiest season of all.

There'll be parties for hosting,
Marshmallows for toasting,
And caroling out in the snow.
There'll be scary ghost stories
And tales of the glories
Of Christmases long, long ago.

It's the most wonderful time of the year.
There'll be much mistltoe-ing, and hearts will
  be glowing
When loved ones are near.
It's the most wonderful time of the year.

It's the most wonderful time of the year.
There'll be much mistltoe-ing, and hearts will
  be glowing
When loved ones are near.
It's the most wonderful time,
It's the most wonderful time,
It's the most wonderful time of the year.

Sleigh Ride

Just hear those sleigh bells jingling,
Ring-ting-tingling, too.
Come on, it's lovely weather
For a sleigh ride together with you.
Outside, the snow is falling,
And friends are calling, "Yoo hoo."
Come on, it's lovely weather
For a sleigh ride together with you.

Giddy-yap, giddy-yap, giddy-yap, let's go!
Let's look at the show.
We're riding in a wonderland of snow.
Giddy-yap, giddy-yap, giddy-yap, it's grand
Just holding your hand.
We're gliding along with the song
Of a wintery fairyland.

Our cheeks are nice and rosy,
And comfy cozy are we.
We're snuggled up together
Like two birds of a feather would be.
Let's take that road before us
And sing a chorus or two.
Come on, it's lovely weather
For a sleigh ride together with you. ❋

There's a birthday party at the home of
  Farmer Gray.
It'll be the perfect ending of a perfect day.
We'll be singing the songs we love to sing
  without a single stop
At the fireplace, while we watch the chestnuts pop.
Pop! Pop! Pop!

There's a happy feeling nothing in the world
  can buy,
When they pass around the coffee and the
  pumpkin pie.
It'll nearly be like a picture print by Currier
  and Ives.
These wonderful things are the things we
  remember all through our lives.

Just hear...
(repeat from beginning to snowflake)

Snowfall

Snowfall, softly, gently drift down.
Snowflakes whisper 'neath my window.
Covering trees misty white,
Velvet breeze 'round my doorstep.
Gently, softly, silent snowfall!

❋　❋　❋　❋　❋　❋　❋　❋　❋　❋　❋

We Need a Little Christmas

Haul out the holly,
Put up the tree before my
Spirit falls again.
Fill up the stocking,
I may be rushing things, but
Deck the halls again now.

For we need a little Christmas,
Right this very minute,
Candles in the window,
Carols at the spinet.
Yes, we need a little Christmas,
Right this very minute,
It hasn't snowed a single flurry,
But Santa, dear, we're in a hurry.

So climb down the chimney,
Turn on the brightest string of
Lights I've ever seen,
Slice up the fruitcake,
It's time we hung some tinsel
On that evergreen bough.

For I've grown a little leaner,
Grown a little colder,
Grown a little sadder,
Grown a little older.
And I need a little angel,
Sitting on my shoulder,
I need a little Christmas now!

For we need a little music,
Need a little laughter,
Need a little singing
Ringing through the rafter.
And we need a little snappy
"Happy ever after,"
We need a little Christmas now!

White Christmas

The sun is shining, the grass is green,
The orange and palm trees sway.
There's never been such a day
In Beverly Hills, L. A.
But it's December the twenty-fourth,
And I am longing to be up north.

I'm dreaming of a white Christmas,
Just like the ones I used to know,
Where the treetops glisten and children listen
To hear sleigh bells in the snow.

I'm dreaming of a white Christmas
With every Christmas card I write:
"May your days be merry and bright
And may all your Christmases be white."

Winter Wonderland

Over the ground lies a mantle of white,
A heaven of diamonds shine down through the night;
Two hearts are thillin' in spite of the chill in the
    weather.

Love knows no season; love knows no clime;
Romance can blossom any old time.
Here in the open, we're walkin' and hopin' together!

Sleigh bells ring, are you list'nin'?
In the lane, snow is glist'nin'.
A beautiful sight, we're happy tonight,
Walkin' in a winter wonderland.
Gone away is the bluebird,
Here to stay is the new bird.
He sings a love song as we go along,
Walkin' in a winter wonderland!

In the meadow we can build a snowman,
And pretend that he is Parson Brown.
He'll say, "Are you married?" We'll say, "No, man!
But you can do the job when you're in town!"
Later on, we'll conspire, as we dream by the fire,
To face unafraid the plans that we made,
Walkin' in a winter wonderland!

Sleigh bells ring, are you list'nin'?
In the lane, snow is glist'nin'.
A beautiful sight, we're happy tonight,
Walkin' in a winter wonderland.
Gone away is the bluebird,
Here to stay is the new bird.
He's singing a song as we go along,
Walkin' in a winter wonderland!

In the meadow we can build a snowman,
And pretend that he's a circus clown.
We'll have lots of fun with Mister Snowman,
Until the other kiddies knock him down!
When it snows, ain't it thrillin',
Though your nose gets a chillin'?
We'll frolic and play the Eskimo way,
Walkin' in a winter wonderland!

Wonderful Christmastime

The mood is right, the spirit's up,
We're here tonight and that's enough.
Simply having a wonderful Christmastime.
Simply having a wonderful Christmastime.

The party's on, the feeling's here
That only comes this time of year.
Simply having a wonderful Christmastime.
Simply having a wonderful Christmastime.

The choir of children sing their song.
Ding dong, ding dong.
Ding dong ding.
Ooh, ooh.
Do do do do do do do.

We're simply having a wonderful Christmastime.
Simply having a wonderful Christmastime.

The word is out about the town,
To lift a glass, oh, don't look down.
Simply having a wonderful Christmastime.
Simply having a wonderful Christmastime.

The choir of children sing their song.
(They practiced all year long.)
Ding dong, ding dong, ding dong,
Ding dong, ding dong, ding dong,
Dong, dong, dong, dong.

The party's on, the spirit's up.
We're here tonight and that's enough.
Simply having a wonderful Christmastime.
We're simply having a wonderful Christmastime.

You're All I Want for Christmas

When Santa comes around at Christmas time
And leaves a lot of cheer at every door,
If he would only grant the wish in my heart
I would never ask for more.

You're all I want for Christmas,
All I want my whole life through.
Each day is just like Christmas
Any time that I'm with you.

You're all I want for Christmas,
And if all my dreams come true,
Then I'll awake on Christmas morning
And find my stocking filled with you.

❆ ❆ ❆ ❆ ❆ ❆ ❆ ❆ ❆ ❆ ❆ ❆

Run, run, reindeer.
Run, run, reindeer.
Oh, run, run, reindeer.
Run, run, reindeer.
He don't miss no one.

And haulin' through the snow at a fright'nin' speed
With a half a dozen deer with Rudy to lead.
He's gotta wear his goggles 'cause the snow
　really flies,
And he's cruisin' every pad with a little surprise.

It's the Little Saint Nick. (Little Saint Nick.)
It's the Little Saint Nick. (Little Saint Nick.)

Ah, Merry Christmas, Saint Nick.
(Christmas comes this time each year.)

A Marshmallow World

It's a marshmallow world in the winter
When the snow comes to cover the ground.
It's the time for play. It's a whipped-cream day.
I wait for it the whole year 'round.

Those are marshmallow clouds being friendly
In the arms of the evergreen trees.
And the sun is red like a pumpkin head.
It's shining so your nose won't freeze.

The world is your snowball, see how it grows.
That's how it goes, whenever it snows.
The world is your snowball, just for a song.
Get out and roll it along.

It's a yum, yummy world made for sweethearts.
Take a walk with your favorite girl.
It's a sugar date, what if spring is late?
In winter it's a marshmallow world.

The Most Wonderful Time of the Year

It's the most wonderful time of the year,
With the kids jingle-belling and everyone
　telling you,
"Be of good cheer."
It's the most wonderful time of the year.

It's the hap-happiest season of all,
With those holiday greetings and gay
　happy meetings,
When friends come to call.
It's the hap-happiest season of all.

There'll be parties for hosting,
Marshmallows for toasting,
And caroling out in the snow.
There'll be scary ghost stories
And tales of the glories
Of Christmases long, long ago.

It's the most wonderful time of the year.
There'll be much mistltoe-ing, and hearts will
　be glowing
When loved ones are near.
It's the most wonderful time of the year.

It's the most wonderful time of the year.
There'll be much mistltoe-ing, and hearts will
　be glowing
When loved ones are near.
It's the most wonderful time,
It's the most wonderful time,
It's the most wonderful time of the year.

Sleigh Ride

Just hear those sleigh bells jingling,
Ring-ting-tingling, too.
Come on, it's lovely weather
For a sleigh ride together with you.
Outside, the snow is falling,
And friends are calling, "Yoo hoo."
Come on, it's lovely weather
For a sleigh ride together with you.

Giddy-yap, giddy-yap, giddy-yap, let's go!
Let's look at the show.
We're riding in a wonderland of snow.
Giddy-yap, giddy-yap, giddy-yap, it's grand
Just holding your hand.
We're gliding along with the song
Of a wintery fairyland.

Our cheeks are nice and rosy,
And comfy cozy are we.
We're snuggled up together
Like two birds of a feather would be.
Let's take that road before us
And sing a chorus or two.
Come on, it's lovely weather
For a sleigh ride together with you. ❄

There's a birthday party at the home of
　Farmer Gray.
It'll be the perfect ending of a perfect day.
We'll be singing the songs we love to sing
　without a single stop
At the fireplace, while we watch the chestnuts pop.
Pop! Pop! Pop!

There's a happy feeling nothing in the world
　can buy,
When they pass around the coffee and the
　pumpkin pie.
It'll nearly be like a picture print by Currier
　and Ives.
These wonderful things are the things we
　remember all through our lives.

Just hear...
(repeat from beginning to snowflake)

Snowfall

Snowfall, softly, gently drift down.
Snowflakes whisper 'neath my window.
Covering trees misty white,
Velvet breeze 'round my doorstep.
Gently, softly, silent snowfall!

❄　❄　❄　❄　❄　❄　❄　❄　❄　❄　❄

We Need a Little Christmas

Haul out the holly,
Put up the tree before my
Spirit falls again.
Fill up the stocking,
I may be rushing things, but
Deck the halls again now.

For we need a little Christmas,
Right this very minute,
Candles in the window,
Carols at the spinet.
Yes, we need a little Christmas,
Right this very minute,
It hasn't snowed a single flurry,
But Santa, dear, we're in a hurry.

So climb down the chimney,
Turn on the brightest string of
Lights I've ever seen,
Slice up the fruitcake,
It's time we hung some tinsel
On that evergreen bough.

For I've grown a little leaner,
Grown a little colder,
Grown a little sadder,
Grown a little older.
And I need a little angel,
Sitting on my shoulder,
I need a little Christmas now!

For we need a little music,
Need a little laughter,
Need a little singing
Ringing through the rafter.
And we need a little snappy
"Happy ever after,"
We need a little Christmas now!

White Christmas

The sun is shining, the grass is green,
The orange and palm trees sway.
There's never been such a day
In Beverly Hills, L. A.
But it's December the twenty-fourth,
And I am longing to be up north.

I'm dreaming of a white Christmas,
Just like the ones I used to know,
Where the treetops glisten and children listen
To hear sleigh bells in the snow.

I'm dreaming of a white Christmas
With every Christmas card I write:
"May your days be merry and bright
And may all your Christmases be white."

Winter Wonderland

Over the ground lies a mantle of white,
A heaven of diamonds shine down through the night;
Two hearts are thillin' in spite of the chill in the
  weather.

Love knows no season; love knows no clime;
Romance can blossom any old time.
Here in the open, we're walkin' and hopin' together!

Sleigh bells ring, are you list'nin'?
In the lane, snow is glist'nin'.
A beautiful sight, we're happy tonight,
Walkin' in a winter wonderland.
Gone away is the bluebird,
Here to stay is the new bird.
He sings a love song as we go along,
Walkin' in a winter wonderland!

In the meadow we can build a snowman,
And pretend that he is Parson Brown.
He'll say, "Are you married?" We'll say, "No, man!
But you can do the job when you're in town!"
Later on, we'll conspire, as we dream by the fire,
To face unafraid the plans that we made,
Walkin' in a winter wonderland!

Sleigh bells ring, are you list'nin'?
In the lane, snow is glist'nin'.
A beautiful sight, we're happy tonight,
Walkin' in a winter wonderland.
Gone away is the bluebird,
Here to stay is the new bird.
He's singing a song as we go along,
Walkin' in a winter wonderland!

In the meadow we can build a snowman,
And pretend that he's a circus clown.
We'll have lots of fun with Mister Snowman,
Until the other kiddies knock him down!
When it snows, ain't it thrillin',
Though your nose gets a chillin'?
We'll frolic and play the Eskimo way,
Walkin' in a winter wonderland!

Wonderful Christmastime

The mood is right, the spirit's up,
We're here tonight and that's enough.
Simply having a wonderful Christmastime.
Simply having a wonderful Christmastime.

The party's on, the feeling's here
That only comes this time of year.
Simply having a wonderful Christmastime.
Simply having a wonderful Christmastime.

The choir of children sing their song.
Ding dong, ding dong.
Ding dong ding.
Ooh, ooh.
Do do do do do do do.

We're simply having a wonderful Christmastime.
Simply having a wonderful Christmastime.

The word is out about the town,
To lift a glass, oh, don't look down.
Simply having a wonderful Christmastime.
Simply having a wonderful Christmastime.

The choir of children sing their song.
(They practiced all year long.)
Ding dong, ding dong, ding dong,
Ding dong, ding dong, ding dong,
Dong, dong, dong, dong.

The party's on, the spirit's up.
We're here tonight and that's enough.
Simply having a wonderful Christmastime.
We're simply having a wonderful Christmastime.

You're All I Want for Christmas

When Santa comes around at Christmas time
And leaves a lot of cheer at every door,
If he would only grant the wish in my heart
I would never ask for more.

You're all I want for Christmas,
All I want my whole life through.
Each day is just like Christmas
Any time that I'm with you.

You're all I want for Christmas,
And if all my dreams come true,
Then I'll awake on Christmas morning
And find my stocking filled with you.

❄ ❄ ❄ ❄ ❄ ❄ ❄ ❄ ❄ ❄ ❄ ❄

Run, run, reindeer.
Run, run, reindeer.
Oh, run, run, reindeer.
Run, run, reindeer.
He don't miss no one.

And haulin' through the snow at a fright'nin' speed
With a half a dozen deer with Rudy to lead.
He's gotta wear his goggles 'cause the snow
 really flies,
And he's cruisin' every pad with a little surprise.

It's the Little Saint Nick. (Little Saint Nick.)
It's the Little Saint Nick. (Little Saint Nick.)

Ah, Merry Christmas, Saint Nick.
(Christmas comes this time each year.)

A Marshmallow World

It's a marshmallow world in the winter
When the snow comes to cover the ground.
It's the time for play. It's a whipped-cream day.
I wait for it the whole year 'round.

Those are marshmallow clouds being friendly
In the arms of the evergreen trees.
And the sun is red like a pumpkin head.
It's shining so your nose won't freeze.

The world is your snowball, see how it grows.
That's how it goes, whenever it snows.
The world is your snowball, just for a song.
Get out and roll it along.

It's a yum, yummy world made for sweethearts.
Take a walk with your favorite girl.
It's a sugar date, what if spring is late?
In winter it's a marshmallow world.

The Most Wonderful Time of the Year

It's the most wonderful time of the year,
With the kids jingle-belling and everyone
 telling you,
"Be of good cheer."
It's the most wonderful time of the year.

It's the hap-happiest season of all,
With those holiday greetings and gay
 happy meetings,
When friends come to call.
It's the hap-happiest season of all.

There'll be parties for hosting,
Marshmallows for toasting,
And caroling out in the snow.
There'll be scary ghost stories
And tales of the glories
Of Christmases long, long ago.

It's the most wonderful time of the year.
There'll be much mistltoe-ing, and hearts will
 be glowing
When loved ones are near.
It's the most wonderful time of the year.

It's the most wonderful time of the year.
There'll be much mistltoe-ing, and hearts will
 be glowing
When loved ones are near.
It's the most wonderful time,
It's the most wonderful time,
It's the most wonderful time of the year.

Sleigh Ride

Just hear those sleigh bells jingling,
Ring-ting-tingling, too.
Come on, it's lovely weather
For a sleigh ride together with you.
Outside, the snow is falling,
And friends are calling, "Yoo hoo."
Come on, it's lovely weather
For a sleigh ride together with you.

Giddy-yap, giddy-yap, giddy-yap, let's go!
Let's look at the show.
We're riding in a wonderland of snow.
Giddy-yap, giddy-yap, giddy-yap, it's grand
Just holding your hand.
We're gliding along with the song
Of a wintery fairyland.

Our cheeks are nice and rosy,
And comfy cozy are we.
We're snuggled up together
Like two birds of a feather would be.
Let's take that road before us
And sing a chorus or two.
Come on, it's lovely weather
For a sleigh ride together with you. ❊

There's a birthday party at the home of
 Farmer Gray.
It'll be the perfect ending of a perfect day.
We'll be singing the songs we love to sing
 without a single stop
At the fireplace, while we watch the chestnuts pop.
Pop! Pop! Pop!

There's a happy feeling nothing in the world
 can buy,
When they pass around the coffee and the
 pumpkin pie.
It'll nearly be like a picture print by Currier
 and Ives.
These wonderful things are the things we
 remember all through our lives.

Just hear...
(repeat from beginning to snowflake)

Snowfall

Snowfall, softly, gently drift down.
Snowflakes whisper 'neath my window.
Covering trees misty white,
Velvet breeze 'round my doorstep.
Gently, softly, silent snowfall!

❊ ❊ ❊ ❊ ❊ ❊ ❊ ❊ ❊ ❊ ❊

We Need a Little Christmas

Haul out the holly,
Put up the tree before my
Spirit falls again.
Fill up the stocking,
I may be rushing things, but
Deck the halls again now.

For we need a little Christmas,
Right this very minute,
Candles in the window,
Carols at the spinet.
Yes, we need a little Christmas,
Right this very minute,
It hasn't snowed a single flurry,
But Santa, dear, we're in a hurry.

So climb down the chimney,
Turn on the brightest string of
Lights I've ever seen,
Slice up the fruitcake,
It's time we hung some tinsel
On that evergreen bough.

For I've grown a little leaner,
Grown a little colder,
Grown a little sadder,
Grown a little older.
And I need a little angel,
Sitting on my shoulder,
I need a little Christmas now!

For we need a little music,
Need a little laughter,
Need a little singing
Ringing through the rafter.
And we need a little snappy
"Happy ever after,"
We need a little Christmas now!

Music and Lyric by Jerry Herman
© 1966 (Renewed) JERRY HERMAN
All Rights Controlled by JERRYCO MUSIC CO.
Exclusive Agent: EDWIN H. MORRIS & COMPANY, A Division of MPL Music
Publishing, Inc.

White Christmas

The sun is shining, the grass is green,
The orange and palm trees sway.
There's never been such a day
In Beverly Hills, L. A.
But it's December the twenty-fourth,
And I am longing to be up north.

I'm dreaming of a white Christmas,
Just like the ones I used to know,
Where the treetops glisten and children listen
To hear sleigh bells in the snow.

I'm dreaming of a white Christmas
With every Christmas card I write:
"May your days be merry and bright
And may all your Christmases be white."

Words and Music by Irving Berlin
© Copyright 1940, 1942 by Irving Berlin
Copyright Renewed

Winter Wonderland

Over the ground lies a mantle of white,
A heaven of diamonds shine down through the night;
Two hearts are thillin' in spite of the chill in the
    weather.

Love knows no season; love knows no clime;
Romance can blossom any old time.
Here in the open, we're walkin' and hopin' together!

Sleigh bells ring, are you list'nin'?
In the lane, snow is glist'nin'.
A beautiful sight, we're happy tonight,
Walkin' in a winter wonderland.
Gone away is the bluebird,
Here to stay is the new bird.
He sings a love song as we go along,
Walkin' in a winter wonderland!

In the meadow we can build a snowman,
And pretend that he is Parson Brown.
He'll say, "Are you married?" We'll say, "No, man!
But you can do the job when you're in town!"
Later on, we'll conspire, as we dream by the fire,
To face unafraid the plans that we made,
Walkin' in a winter wonderland!

Sleigh bells ring, are you list'nin'?
In the lane, snow is glist'nin'.
A beautiful sight, we're happy tonight,
Walkin' in a winter wonderland.
Gone away is the bluebird,
Here to stay is the new bird.
He's singing a song as we go along,
Walkin' in a winter wonderland!

In the meadow we can build a snowman,
And pretend that he's a circus clown.
We'll have lots of fun with Mister Snowman,
Until the other kiddies knock him down!
When it snows, ain't it thrillin',
Though your nose gets a chillin'?
We'll frolic and play the Eskimo way,
Walkin' in a winter wonderland!

Words by Dick Smith
Music by Felix Bernard
© 1934 (Renewed) WB MUSIC CORP.
All Rights in Canada Administered by REDWOOD MUSIC LTD.

Wonderful Christmastime

The mood is right, the spirit's up,
We're here tonight and that's enough.
Simply having a wonderful Christmastime.
Simply having a wonderful Christmastime.

The party's on, the feeling's here
That only comes this time of year.
Simply having a wonderful Christmastime.
Simply having a wonderful Christmastime.

The choir of children sing their song.
Ding dong, ding dong.
Ding dong ding.
Ooh, ooh.
Do do do do do do do.

We're simply having a wonderful Christmastime.
Simply having a wonderful Christmastime.

The word is out about the town,
To lift a glass, oh, don't look down.
Simply having a wonderful Christmastime.
Simply having a wonderful Christmastime.

The choir of children sing their song.
(They practiced all year long.)
Ding dong, ding dong, ding dong,
Ding dong, ding dong, ding dong,
Dong, dong, dong, dong.

The party's on, the spirit's up.
We're here tonight and that's enough.
Simply having a wonderful Christmastime.
We're simply having a wonderful Christmastime.

Words and Music by Paul McCartney
© 1979 MPL COMMUNICATIONS LTD.
Administered by MPL COMMUNICATIONS, INC.

You're All I Want for Christmas

When Santa comes around at Christmas time
And leaves a lot of cheer at every door,
If he would only grant the wish in my heart
I would never ask for more.

You're all I want for Christmas,
All I want my whole life through.
Each day is just like Christmas
Any time that I'm with you.

You're all I want for Christmas,
And if all my dreams come true,
Then I'll awake on Christmas morning
And find my stocking filled with you.

Words and Music by Glen Moore and Seger Ellis
Copyright © 1948 SONGS OF UNIVERSAL, INC.
Copyright Renewed

❄ ❄ ❄ ❄ ❄ ❄ ❄ ❄ ❄ ❄ ❄ ❄

Run, run, reindeer.
Run, run, reindeer.
Oh, run, run, reindeer.
Run, run, reindeer.
He don't miss no one.

And haulin' through the snow at a fright'nin' speed
With a half a dozen deer with Rudy to lead.
He's gotta wear his goggles 'cause the snow
  really flies,
And he's cruisin' every pad with a little surprise.

It's the Little Saint Nick. (Little Saint Nick.)
It's the Little Saint Nick. (Little Saint Nick.)

Ah, Merry Christmas, Saint Nick.
(Christmas comes this time each year.)

A Marshmallow World

It's a marshmallow world in the winter
When the snow comes to cover the ground.
It's the time for play. It's a whipped-cream day.
I wait for it the whole year 'round.

Those are marshmallow clouds being friendly
In the arms of the evergreen trees.
And the sun is red like a pumpkin head.
It's shining so your nose won't freeze.

The world is your snowball, see how it grows.
That's how it goes, whenever it snows.
The world is your snowball, just for a song.
Get out and roll it along.

It's a yum, yummy world made for sweethearts.
Take a walk with your favorite girl.
It's a sugar date, what if spring is late?
In winter it's a marshmallow world.

The Most Wonderful Time of the Year

It's the most wonderful time of the year,
With the kids jingle-belling and everyone
  telling you,
"Be of good cheer."
It's the most wonderful time of the year.

It's the hap-happiest season of all,
With those holiday greetings and gay
  happy meetings,
When friends come to call.
It's the hap-happiest season of all.

There'll be parties for hosting,
Marshmallows for toasting,
And caroling out in the snow.
There'll be scary ghost stories
And tales of the glories
Of Christmases long, long ago.

It's the most wonderful time of the year.
There'll be much mistltoe-ing, and hearts will
  be glowing
When loved ones are near.
It's the most wonderful time of the year.

It's the most wonderful time of the year.
There'll be much mistltoe-ing, and hearts will
  be glowing
When loved ones are near.
It's the most wonderful time,
It's the most wonderful time,
It's the most wonderful time of the year.

Sleigh Ride

Just hear those sleigh bells jingling,
Ring-ting-tingling, too.
Come on, it's lovely weather
For a sleigh ride together with you.
Outside, the snow is falling,
And friends are calling, "Yoo hoo."
Come on, it's lovely weather
For a sleigh ride together with you.

Giddy-yap, giddy-yap, giddy-yap, let's go!
Let's look at the show.
We're riding in a wonderland of snow.
Giddy-yap, giddy-yap, giddy-yap, it's grand
Just holding your hand.
We're gliding along with the song
Of a wintery fairyland.

Our cheeks are nice and rosy,
And comfy cozy are we.
We're snuggled up together
Like two birds of a feather would be.
Let's take that road before us
And sing a chorus or two.
Come on, it's lovely weather
For a sleigh ride together with you. ❊

There's a birthday party at the home of
  Farmer Gray.
It'll be the perfect ending of a perfect day.
We'll be singing the songs we love to sing
  without a single stop
At the fireplace, while we watch the chestnuts pop.
Pop! Pop! Pop!

There's a happy feeling nothing in the world
  can buy,
When they pass around the coffee and the
  pumpkin pie.
It'll nearly be like a picture print by Currier
  and Ives.
These wonderful things are the things we
  remember all through our lives.

Just hear...
(repeat from beginning to snowflake)

Snowfall

Snowfall, softly, gently drift down.
Snowflakes whisper 'neath my window.
Covering trees misty white,
Velvet breeze 'round my doorstep.
Gently, softly, silent snowfall!

❊ ❊ ❊ ❊ ❊ ❊ ❊ ❊ ❊ ❊ ❊

We Need a Little Christmas

Haul out the holly,
Put up the tree before my
Spirit falls again.
Fill up the stocking,
I may be rushing things, but
Deck the halls again now.

For we need a little Christmas,
Right this very minute,
Candles in the window,
Carols at the spinet.
Yes, we need a little Christmas,
Right this very minute,
It hasn't snowed a single flurry,
But Santa, dear, we're in a hurry.

So climb down the chimney,
Turn on the brightest string of
Lights I've ever seen,
Slice up the fruitcake,
It's time we hung some tinsel
On that evergreen bough.

For I've grown a little leaner,
Grown a little colder,
Grown a little sadder,
Grown a little older.
And I need a little angel,
Sitting on my shoulder,
I need a little Christmas now!

For we need a little music,
Need a little laughter,
Need a little singing
Ringing through the rafter.
And we need a little snappy
"Happy ever after,"
We need a little Christmas now!

White Christmas

The sun is shining, the grass is green,
The orange and palm trees sway.
There's never been such a day
In Beverly Hills, L. A.
But it's December the twenty-fourth,
And I am longing to be up north.

I'm dreaming of a white Christmas,
Just like the ones I used to know,
Where the treetops glisten and children listen
To hear sleigh bells in the snow.

I'm dreaming of a white Christmas
With every Christmas card I write:
"May your days be merry and bright
And may all your Christmases be white."

Winter Wonderland

Over the ground lies a mantle of white,
A heaven of diamonds shine down through the night;
Two hearts are thillin' in spite of the chill in the
   weather.

Love knows no season; love knows no clime;
Romance can blossom any old time.
Here in the open, we're walkin' and hopin' together!

Sleigh bells ring, are you list'nin'?
In the lane, snow is glist'nin'.
A beautiful sight, we're happy tonight,
Walkin' in a winter wonderland.
Gone away is the bluebird,
Here to stay is the new bird.
He sings a love song as we go along,
Walkin' in a winter wonderland!

In the meadow we can build a snowman,
And pretend that he is Parson Brown.
He'll say, "Are you married?" We'll say, "No, man!
But you can do the job when you're in town!"
Later on, we'll conspire, as we dream by the fire,
To face unafraid the plans that we made,
Walkin' in a winter wonderland!

Sleigh bells ring, are you list'nin'?
In the lane, snow is glist'nin'.
A beautiful sight, we're happy tonight,
Walkin' in a winter wonderland.
Gone away is the bluebird,
Here to stay is the new bird.
He's singing a song as we go along,
Walkin' in a winter wonderland!

In the meadow we can build a snowman,
And pretend that he's a circus clown.
We'll have lots of fun with Mister Snowman,
Until the other kiddies knock him down!
When it snows, ain't it thrillin',
Though your nose gets a chillin'?
We'll frolic and play the Eskimo way,
Walkin' in a winter wonderland!

Wonderful Christmastime

The mood is right, the spirit's up,
We're here tonight and that's enough.
Simply having a wonderful Christmastime.
Simply having a wonderful Christmastime.

The party's on, the feeling's here
That only comes this time of year.
Simply having a wonderful Christmastime.
Simply having a wonderful Christmastime.

The choir of children sing their song.
Ding dong, ding dong.
Ding dong ding.
Ooh, ooh.
Do do do do do do do.

We're simply having a wonderful Christmastime.
Simply having a wonderful Christmastime.

The word is out about the town,
To lift a glass, oh, don't look down.
Simply having a wonderful Christmastime.
Simply having a wonderful Christmastime.

The choir of children sing their song.
(They practiced all year long.)
Ding dong, ding dong, ding dong,
Ding dong, ding dong, ding dong,
Dong, dong, dong, dong.

The party's on, the spirit's up.
We're here tonight and that's enough.
Simply having a wonderful Christmastime.
We're simply having a wonderful Christmastime.

You're All I Want for Christmas

When Santa comes around at Christmas time
And leaves a lot of cheer at every door,
If he would only grant the wish in my heart
I would never ask for more.

You're all I want for Christmas,
All I want my whole life through.
Each day is just like Christmas
Any time that I'm with you.

You're all I want for Christmas,
And if all my dreams come true,
Then I'll awake on Christmas morning
And find my stocking filled with you.

❄ ❄ ❄ ❄ ❄ ❄ ❄ ❄ ❄ ❄ ❄

SNOWFALL

Lyrics by RUTH THORNHILL
Music by CLAUDE THORNHILL

THE MOST WONDERFUL TIME OF THE YEAR

Words and Music by EDDIE POLA
and GEORGE WYLE

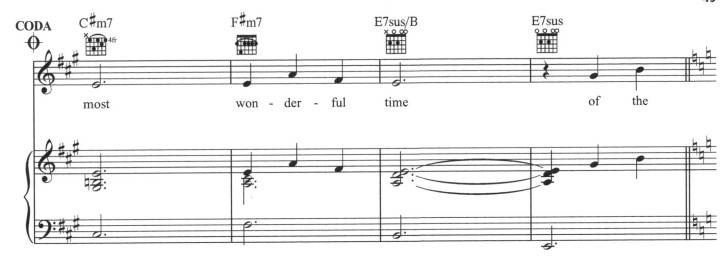

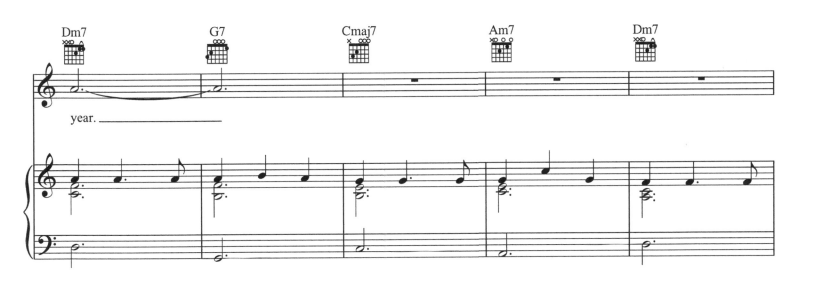

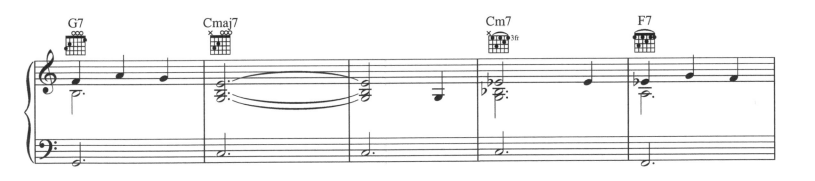

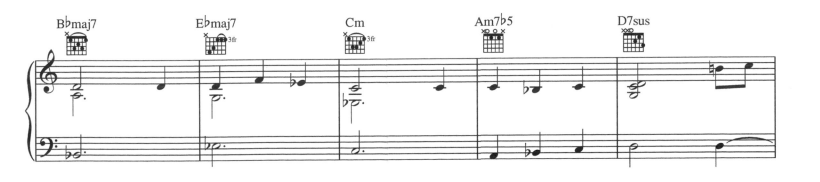

SLEIGH RIDE

Music by LEROY ANDERSON
Words by MITCHELL PARISH

WE NEED A LITTLE CHRISTMAS

from MAME

Music and Lyric by
JERRY HERMAN

WINTER WONDERLAND

Words by DICK SMITH
Music by FELIX BERNARD

WHITE CHRISTMAS

from the Motion Picture Irving Berlin's HOLIDAY INN

Words and Music by
IRVING BERLIN

WONDERFUL CHRISTMASTIME

Words and Music by
PAUL McCARTNEY

The mood is right, ___ the spir-it's up, ___
The par-ty's on, ___ the feel-ing's here ___
The word is out ___ a-bout the town ___

we're here to-night ___ and that's e-nough. ___
that on-ly comes ___ this time of year. ___
to lift a glass, ___ oh, don't look down. ___

Sim - ply hav - ing a won-der-ful Christ-mas - time.

YOU'RE ALL I WANT FOR CHRISTMAS

Words and Music by GLEN MOORE
and SEGER ELLIS

Christmas Collections
from Hal Leonard
All books arranged for piano, voice & guitar.

All-Time Christmas Favorites – Second Edition
This second edition features an all-star lineup of 32 Christmas classics, including: Blue Christmas • The Chipmunk Song • The Christmas Song • Frosty the Snow Man • Here Comes Santa Claus • I Saw Mommy Kissing Santa Claus • Jingle-Bell Rock • Let It Snow! Let It Snow! Let It Snow! • Merry Christmas, Darling • Nuttin' for Christmas • Rockin' Around the Christmas Tree • Rudolph the Red-Nosed Reindeer • Santa, Bring My Baby Back (To Me) • There Is No Christmas like a Home Christmas • and more.
00359051...$14.99

The Best Christmas Songs Ever – 6th Edition
69 all-time favorites are included in the 6th edition of this collection of Christmas tunes. Includes: Auld Lang Syne • Coventry Carol • Frosty the Snow Man • Happy Holiday • It Came Upon the Midnight Clear • O Holy Night • Rudolph the Red-Nosed Reindeer • Silver Bells • What Child Is This? • and many more.
00359130...$24.99

The Big Book of Christmas Songs – 2nd Edition
An outstanding collection of over 120 all-time Christmas favorites and hard-to-find classics. Features: Angels We Have Heard on High • As Each Happy Christmas • Auld Lang Syne • The Boar's Head Carol • Christ Was Born on Christmas Day • Bring a Torch Jeannette, Isabella • Carol of the Bells • Coventry Carol • Deck the Halls • The First Noel • The Friendly Beasts • God Rest Ye Merry Gentlemen • I Heard the Bells on Christmas Day • It Came Upon a Midnight Clear • Jesu, Joy of Man's Desiring • Joy to the World • Masters in This Hall • O Holy Night • The Story of the Shepherd • 'Twas the Night Before Christmas • What Child Is This? • and many more. Includes guitar chord frames.
00311520...$19.95

Christmas Songs – Budget Books
Save some money this Christmas with this fabulous budget-priced collection of 100 holiday favorites: All I Want for Christmas Is You • Christmas Time Is Here • Feliz Navidad • Grandma Got Run Over by a Reindeer • Happy Holiday • I'll Be Home for Christmas • Jesus Born on This Day • Last Christmas • Merry Christmas, Baby • O Holy Night • Please Come Home for Christmas • Rockin' Around the Christmas Tree • Some Children See Him • We Need a Little Christmas • What Child Is This? • and more.
00310887...$12.99

The Definitive Christmas Collection – 3rd Edition
Revised with even more Christmas classics, this must-have 3rd edition contains 127 top songs, such as: Blue Christmas • Christmas Time Is Here • Do You Hear What I Hear • The First Noel • A Holly Jolly Christmas • Jingle-Bell Rock • Little Saint Nick • Merry Christmas, Darling • O Holy Night • Rudolph, the Red-Nosed Reindeer • Silver and Gold • We Need a Little Christmas • You're All I Want for Christmas • and more!
00311602...$24.95

Essential Songs – Christmas
Over 100 essential holiday favorites: Blue Christmas • The Christmas Song • Deck the Hall • Frosty the Snow Man • A Holly Jolly Christmas • I'll Be Home for Christmas • Joy to the World • Let It Snow! Let It Snow! Let It Snow! • My Favorite Things • Rudolph the Red-Nosed Reindeer • Silver Bells • and more!
00311241...$24.95

The Muppet Christmas Carol
Matching folio to the blockbuster movie featuring 11 Muppet carols and eight pages of color photos. Bless Us All • Chairman of the Board • Christmas Scat • Finale - When Love Is Found/It Feels like Christmas • It Feels like Christmas • Marley and Marley • One More Sleep 'Til Christmas • Room in Your Heart • Scrooge • Thankful Heart • When Love Is Gone.
00312483...$14.95

Tim Burton's The Nightmare Before Christmas
This book features 11 songs from Tim Burton's creepy animated classic, with music and lyrics by Danny Elfman. Songs include: Jack's Lament • Jack's Obsession • Kidnap the Sandy Claws • Making Christmas • Oogie Boogie's Song • Poor Jack • Sally's Song • This Is Halloween • Town Meeting Song • What's This? • Finale/Reprise.
00312488...$12.99

Ultimate Christmas – 3rd Edition
100 seasonal favorites: Auld Lang Syne • Bring a Torch, Jeannette, Isabella • Carol of the Bells • The Chipmunk Song • Christmas Time Is Here • The First Noel • Frosty the Snow Man • Gesù Bambino • Happy Holiday • Happy Xmas (War Is Over) • Hymne • Jesu, Joy of Man's Desiring • Jingle-Bell Rock • March of the Toys • My Favorite Things • The Night Before Christmas Song • Pretty Paper • Silver and Gold • Silver Bells • Suzy Snowflake • What Child Is This • The Wonderful World of Christmas • and more.
00361399 ....$19.95

pro vocal® BETTER THAN KARAOKE!

Pro Vocal® Series
SONGBOOK & SOUND-ALIKE CD
SING GREAT SONGS WITH A PROFESSIONAL BAND

Whether you're a karaoke singer or an auditioning professional, the Pro Vocal® series is for you! Unlike most karaoke packs, each book in the Pro Vocal Series contains the lyrics, melody, and chord symbols for at least eight hit songs. The CD contains demos for listening, and separate backing tracks so you can sing along. The CD is playable on any CD player, but it is also enhanced so PC and Mac computer users can adjust the recording to any pitch without changing the tempo! Perfect for home rehearsal, parties, auditions, corporate events, and gigs without a backup band.

WOMEN'S EDITIONS

MEN'S EDITIONS

WARM-UPS

MIXED EDITIONS

These editions feature songs for both male and female voices.

KIDS EDITIONS

Visit Hal Leonard online at
www.halleonard.com

HAL•LEONARD®

7777 W. BLUEMOUND RD. P.O. BOX 13819 MILWAUKEE, WI 53213

Prices, contents, & availability subject to change without notice.

1113

SING WITH THE CHOIR

CD INCLUDED

These **GREAT COLLECTIONS** let singers
BECOME PART OF A FULL CHOIR and sing along
with some of the most-loved songs of all time.

Each book includes SATB parts (arrangements are enlarged from octavo-size to 9" x 12")
and the accompanying CD features full, professionally recorded performances.

Now you just need to turn on the CD, open the book, pick your part, and
SING ALONG WITH THE CHOIR!

1. ANDREW LLOYD WEBBER
Any Dream Will Do • As If We Never Said Goodbye • Don't Cry for Me Argentina • Love Changes Everything • Memory • The Music of the Night • Pie Jesu • Whistle down the Wind.
00333001 Book/CD Pack $14.95

2. BROADWAY
Bring Him Home • Cabaret • For Good • Luck Be a Lady • Seasons of Love • There's No Business like Show Business • Where Is Love? • You'll Never Walk Alone.
00333002 Book/CD Pack $14.95

3. STANDARDS
Cheek to Cheek • Georgia on My Mind • I Left My Heart in San Francisco • I'm Beginning to See the Light • Moon River • On the Sunny Side of the Street • Skylark • When I Fall in Love.
00333003 Book/CD Pack $14.95

4. THE 1950s
At the Hop • The Great Pretender • Kansas City • La Bamba • Love Me Tender • My Prayer • Rock Around the Clock • Unchained Melody.
00333004 Book/CD Pack $14.95

5. THE 1960s
All You Need is Love • Can't Help Falling in Love • Dancing in the Street • Good Vibrations • I Heard It Through the Grapevine • I'm a Believer • Under the Boardwalk • What a Wonderful World.
00333005 Book/CD Pack $14.95

6. THE 1970s
Ain't No Mountain High Enough • Bohemian Rhapsody • I'll Be There • Imagine • Let It Be • Night Fever • Yesterday Once More • You Are the Sunshine of My Life.
00333006 Book/CD Pack $14.95

7. DISNEY FAVORITES
The Bare Necessities • Be Our Guest • Circle of Life • Cruella De Vil • Friend like Me • Hakuna Matata • Joyful, Joyful • Under the Sea.
00333007 Book/CD Pack $14.95

8. DISNEY HITS
Beauty and the Beast • Breaking Free • Can You Feel the Love Tonight • Candle on the Water • Colors of the Wind • A Whole New World (Aladdin's Theme) • You'll Be in My Heart • You've Got a Friend in Me.
00333008 Book/CD Pack $14.95

9. LES MISÉRABLES
At the End of the Day • Bring Him Home • Castle on a Cloud • Do You Hear the People Sing? • Finale • I Dreamed a Dream • On My Own • One Day More.
00333009 Book/CD Pack $14.99

10. CHRISTMAS FAVORITES
Frosty the Snow Man • The Holiday Season • (There's No Place Like) Home for the Holidays • Little Saint Nick • Merry Christmas, Darling • Santa Claus Is Comin' to Town • Silver Bells • White Christmas.
00333011 Book/CD Pack $14.95

11. CHRISTMAS TIME IS HERE
Blue Christmas • Christmas Time is Here • Feliz Navidad • Happy Xmas (War Is Over) • I'll Be Home for Christmas • Let It Snow! Let It Snow! Let It Snow! • We Need a Little Christmas • Wonderful Christmastime.
00333012 Book/CD Pack $14.95

12. THE SOUND OF MUSIC
Climb Ev'ry Mountain • Do-Re-Mi • Edelweiss • The Lonely Goatherd • My Favorite Things • So Long, Farewell • The Sound of Music.
00333019 Book/CD Pack $14.99

13. CHRISTMAS CAROLS
Angels We Have Heard on High • Deck the Hall • Go, Tell It on the Mountain • Joy to the World • O Come, All Ye Faithful (Adeste Fideles) • O Holy Night • Silent Night • We Wish You a Merry Christmas.
00333020 Book/CD Pack $14.99

14. GLEE
Can't Fight This Feeling • Don't Stop Believin' • Jump • Keep Holding On • Lean on Me • No Air • Rehab • Somebody to Love.
00333059 Book/CD Pack $16.99

15. HYMNS
Abide with Me • All Hail the Power of Jesus' Name • Amazing Grace • Be Still My Soul • Blessed Assurance • The Church's One Foundation • Come, Thou Almighty King • It Is Well with My Soul.
00333158 Book/CD Pack $14.99

16. WORSHIP
All Hail the Power of Jesus' Name • And Can It Be That I Should Gain • Everlasting God • Glory to God Forever • Here I Am to Worship • How Great Is Our God • I Will Rise • A Mighty Fortress Is Our God • My Jesus, I Love Thee • Shout to the Lord • You Are My King (Amazing Love) • Your Name.
00333170 Book/CD Pack $14.99

17. MORE SONGS FROM GLEE
Empire State of Mind • Firework • Hello, Goodbye • Like a Prayer • Lucky • The Safety Dance • Teenage Dream • To Sir, with Love.
00333377 Book/CD Pack $17.99

FOR MORE INFORMATION, SEE YOUR LOCAL MUSIC DEALER, OR WRITE TO:

HAL•LEONARD® CORPORATION
7777 W. BLUEMOUND RD. P.O. BOX 13819 MILWAUKEE, WI 53213

Prices, contents, and availability subject to change without notice.

0212